PUFFIN BOOKS
SWAMI VIVEKANANDA

Dr Devika Rangachari has won several awards for her children's writing. Her book, *Growing Up* (Children's Book Trust, 2000) was on the Honour List of the International Board on Books for Young People (IBBY) in 2002. Her other books include *Harsha Vardhana* (Scholastic, 2009), *The Merry Mischief of Gopal Bhand* (Scholastic, 2007), *The Wit of Tenali Raman* (Scholastic, 2007), *When Amma Went Away* (CBT, 2002) and *Stories from Rajatarangini—Tales of Kashmir* (CBT, 2001). Devika helps to run the Children's Book Forum at the India Habitat Centre, New Delhi. She is currently engaged in post-doctoral research in Indian history. She is also excessively fond of books and chocolates and not necessarily in that order!

Other books in the *Puffin Lives* series

Mother Teresa: Apostle of Love
by Rukmini Chawla
Jawaharlal Nehru: The Jewel of India
by Aditi De
Ashoka: The Great and Compassionate King
by Subhadra Sen Gupta
Rani Lakshmibai: The Valiant Queen of Jhansi
by Deepa Agarwal
Akbar: The Mighty Emperor
by Kavitha Mandana
Mahatma Gandhi: The Father of the Nation
by Subhadra Sen Gupta
Subhas Chandra Bose: The Great Freedom Fighter
by Anu Kumar
Gautama Buddha: Lord of Wisdom
by Rohini Chowdhury
The 14th Dalai Lama: Buddha of Compassion
by Aravinda Anantharaman
Guru Nanak: The Enlightened Master
by Sreelata Menon

SWAMI

Vivekananda

A MAN WITH
A VISION

DEVIKA RANGACHARI

PUFFIN BOOKS
An imprint of Penguin Random House

PUFFIN BOOKS

USA | Canada | UK | Ireland | Australia
New Zealand | India | South Africa | China | Singapore

Puffin Books is part of the Penguin Random House group of companies
whose addresses can be found at global.penguinrandomhouse.com

Published by Penguin Random House India Pvt. Ltd
4th Floor, Capital Tower 1, MG Road,
Gurugram 122 002, Haryana, India

First published in puffin by penguin books india 2011

Copyright © Devika Rangachari 2011

10 9 8 7 6 5 4 3 2

ISBN 9780143331865

Typeset in bembo by Eleven Arts, Delhi
Printed at Manipal Technologies Limited, India

www.penguin.co.in

MIX
Paper | Supporting
responsible forestry
FSC® C043100

Contents

1   The Man Behind the Face

Sometimes photographs conceal as much as they reveal. If you look at a photograph of Swami Vivekananda, a man with big eyes and an intense gaze stares back at you. He has a determined jaw; his expression is stern, serious and purposeful. His posture, meanwhile, exudes confidence and strength. You can readily believe that this was the man who revived Hinduism and gave it—and India—an important status in the world scenario. This at a time when India was under British rule when years of political, economic and social exploitation had eroded the confidence and self-respect of her people.

The clear, intelligent eyes—the most arresting feature of his face—belonged to a genius, someone who could speak with passion and brilliance, in such logically sound arguments, that his listeners were mesmerized. This was a man who would not accept anything unless he had reasoned it out for himself. He could be stubborn to the point of exasperation but would not yield his stance once he was convinced of it. He was blunt, frank and straightforward—someone who had no qualms in speaking his mind.

Yet there is also a lot that the photo does not tell you: this was a man who had such a great sense of humour that he would keep his companions entertained for hours on end with his jokes and mimicry. This was also someone who loved playing with children and would happily roll in the mud, laughing and shouting, getting himself dirty and muddy during some vigorous game or the other. This was someone who loved ice-cream so passionately that he would sometimes postpone meetings if he knew it was about to be served! And this was someone who wrote beautifully emotive letters in English, Bengali, Sanskrit and French with equal fluency, documenting his innermost thoughts, dreams, plans, passions and sufferings.

Vivekananda was a great Indian patriot and hero who restored to the Indians, and particularly to the youth, a feeling of self-confidence and pride in their inheritance. He showed the world that Hinduism was a religion of great antiquity and dignity and not 'a world of darkness' as commonly portrayed at the time. He was a strong supporter of the weak and downtrodden among the Indian masses, and of women. He was also a refined spiritual philosopher who preached Vedanta—the school of thought that believes in the oneness of all creations—as the future universal religion.

This remarkable personality, who was to become a saint, a teacher, a leader, a philosopher, a social activist and many other things at the same time, was one of seven children born to a Bengali Hindu couple, Bisvanath Datta, a lawyer in Kolkata (then Calcutta), and his wife, Bhubaneswari Devi. The Datta's first-born, a son, had passed away while an infant. Among the four girls in the family, Haramoni and Swarnamayee were older than Vivekananda, and Kiranbala and Jogendrabala were younger. Mahendranath and Bhupendranath were Vivekananda's two younger brothers. Incidentally, Bhupendranath, the youngest of the siblings, later wrote a biography of his famous brother, entitled *Swami Vivekananda Patriot-Prophet—A Study*, which provides many details of his family life that are not known from any other source.

Vivekananda was born on 12 January 1863 in the Simulia district of north Kolkata. It was the day of *makara sankranti*, the Hindu festival when millions of devotees bathe in the river Ganga. Bhubaneswari Devi had prayed to Shiva for a son after the birth of her first two daughters and this baby was an answer to her prayers. Hence, he was named Vireshwara, one of the many names of Shiva. However, his family also gave him the name Narendranath, which later became Narendra or Naren.

Bisvanath Datta had a thriving practice at the Kolkata High Court. He had also inherited considerable wealth from his ancestors and this enabled the Dattas to lead an extremely comfortable life with many servants, fine clothes and luxuries. Naren's great-grandfather, Rammohan Datta, had been the managing clerk and associate of an English lawyer. One of his two sons, Durgaprasad, who was Bisvanath's father, also showed an inclination for and understanding of law. Hence, Naren was born into a family of three generations of highly successful, wealthy and respected lawyers.

However, in an unexpected turn of events, Naren's grandfather, Durgaprasad, renounced the world when he was just twenty-five years old, despite having a wife, Shyamasundari, and a son, Bisvanath. He left for Varanasi, and Shyamasundari now dedicated herself to bringing up Bisvanath and ensuring that he did not feel his father's absence. Nothing was seen or heard of Durgaprasad thereafter. Naren was to later renounce the world at about the same age as his grandfather.

Naren grew up to be an intelligent but extremely restless child and was often uncontrollable when in the grip of a sudden burst of energy. His mother soon found a way to control and calm him. She would pour a pot of cold water over his head, reciting Shiva's name repeatedly till he became quiet. She once exclaimed to Shiva, 'I had asked you for a son, and you have sent me one of your demons instead!'

Like Shyamasundari, Bhubaneswari Devi, too, was a woman of strong character. Loving and caring, she managed the large household with efficiency, and commanded the respect of everyone who met her. She was small in stature but was known to carry herself like a queen. Vivekananda remarked in later years, 'The love which my mother gave to me has made me what I am and I owe a debt to her that I can never repay.'

Bhubaneswari Devi was a tremendous influence in moulding Naren's personality and on his life in general. He received his early education from her, learning the Bengali alphabet and his first English words, as well as stories from the two epics, the Ramayana and the

Mahabharata. Naren loved these stories and once even stayed in a banana grove for a long time hoping to see Hanuman, for he had heard that this was one of his favourite haunts.

On one occasion, when the child Naren was treated unfairly at school, his mother is supposed to have told him, 'Always follow the truth without caring for the result. Very often you may have to suffer injustice or unpleasant consequences for holding to the truth; but you must not, under any circumstances, abandon it.' This lesson struck home and was followed tenaciously by Naren all through his life. Once, he told an audience: 'I am indebted to my mother for whatever knowledge I have acquired.'

Many years later in December 1894, when Vivekananda's words were making waves around the world, Bhubaneswari Devi received a letter from some women in Massachusetts, America. They had supported his cause and, in the letter, spoke of the debt Vivekananda owed her and which he was eager to acknowledge publicly. They wrote, 'His (Vivekananda's) service to men, women and children in our midst was laid at your feet by him the other day in an address he gave us on the ideals of "Motherhood in India". The worship of his mother will be to all who heard him an inspiration and uplift. Accept, dear Madam, our grateful recognition of your life and work in and through your son.'

Naren's father, Bisvanath Datta, on the other hand, believed that music and poetry were essential to life. One of the many things that Naren inherited from his father was his melodious voice and deep interest in music. He was also trained in classical music on his father's insistence. Bisvanath was a linguist and knew Persian and Arabic. He would recite verses from the Bible, from the works of Persian poet Hafiz and from Sanskrit texts with ease. He also encouraged Naren to read the Bible and *Dewan-i-Hafiz* to become acquainted with different strands of religious thought.

Predictably, Bisvanath's liberal attitude in this regard in those times invited some amount of criticism. In his biography of Vivekananda, his brother, Bhupendranath, notes that their father 'was a product of the old Hindu–Muslim civilization and the new English culture spreading in his time.' Bhupendranath adds, 'That he (Bisvanath) was a respecter of the Bible and of *Dewan-i-Hafiz* has been a matter of adverse criticism of my father ... The writer is grateful to his father for bringing him along with his brothers out of the grip of priestly superstitions and pointing out to them a new life suited to the changing times. This helped the offspring of Bisvanath to become radicals in their ways of thinking.'

Discussions on history, philosophy and religion were a regular feature of the Datta household. Bisvanath would invite his friends to these lively gatherings and Naren, though a small boy, was not excluded from them. Bisvanath often gently encouraged his son to take part in these debates. This helped Naren to broaden his horizons and develop argumentative skills over the years. 'To my father,' once remarked Vivekananda, 'I owe my intellect and compassion.'

Naren learned another lesson in an indirect way through his father's law practice. Insatiably curious and observant, he had noticed that different hookahs (tobacco pipes) were provided in his father's office for clients of different castes. A separate one was kept for Muslims as well. This greatly intrigued Naren who decided to smoke them all in turn to see what would happen. Though the consequences appeared to be minor then, they were actually momentous in the long run. Naren managed to smoke the different pipes but was caught in the act and scolded (it is not clear by whom). His only response was, 'I don't see any difference.' Later, as Vivekananda, he was to completely reject caste as a basis for diffcrentiating between people.

Bisvanath was also generous to a fault and often reckless in sharing his wealth. Many of his relatives were financially supported by him. They lived in his large home, taking advantage of his kind-heartedness. Some of them were drunkards and when Naren grew older, he protested against this situation to his father. Bisvanath told him that there was much misery in the world that Naren was unaware of and that if those who he helped out wanted to forget their pain by drinking, then there was no harm in it. Yet, ironically, Bisvanath kept a very strict eye on his children, ensuring that they followed disciplined routines.

Once when Bisvanath was more reckless than usual in distributing gifts, Naren asked him, 'Father, what are you going to leave me?' Bisvanath answered, 'Go, stand before the mirror and you will see what I leave you.' His words were prophetic in a sense. His son did not need anything more than his intellect and determination to become one of the most famous personalities of modern India.

The Company and the Crown
In 1857, after the Indian rebellion against the British (which is also sometimes referred to as the First War of Independence), the rule of the British East India Company, that was primarily a trading organization, was transferred to the British Crown in the person of Queen Victoria. This was six years before Vivekananda was born. Queen Victoria was later proclaimed Empress of India. Kolkata became the capital of British India and remained so till 1912 when the capital was shifted to Delhi. British rule over the Indian subcontinent lasted till 1947.

2 Boyhood Saga

The grove was thick with many tall trees. Their twisted branches formed a canopy under which the boys could play. It was ideal for secret games: for hiding from and spying on each other. Later, the boys would lie flat on their backs, fingers trailing through the soft, springy grass as they squinted up at the sky through the leafy roof. Then they would jump up once again and throw themselves with much vigour into another game.

But now, their leader wanted to play something different and the boys weren't so sure about this new game. However, they were accustomed to doing what he said for he was tough and hefty, had more energy and enthusiasm than all of them put together, and could play and run and climb for hours on end without tiring, while the others were gasping and pleading for rest. Besides—and this was what really mattered—there was something in the way he spoke and looked at them that had them scurrying to do his bidding. In fact, when they played at being kings and courtiers, he would always be the king; no one was as good or as natural as him in that role. He would sit on a tussock of grass and calmly assign parts to the others. Such was his air of command that none would dream of questioning him but did as he ordered quite willingly.

Yet today was different. He did not want to run around and play but to sit in the grove with his eyes closed.

'But what will you *do*?' exclaimed one boy, who couldn't believe that his friend would want to spend their precious playing time in such a boring manner.

'I am going to close my eyes and think,' was the reply.

The boys fidgeted for a while but their irritated murmurs soon drew to a close and a puzzled silence fell among them as they surveyed their friend. He didn't seem to be aware of them; his eyes were shut tightly as if he were asleep and he looked like he was going to sit like that for a long time.

'I think he is meditating,' said one uncertainly. 'But why would he want to do this instead of playing?'

It was a mystery, and they stood for a long time hopping from leg to leg, trying to solve it. They might have stood there longer had a sudden rustle in the thick grass not drawn the attention of the boy nearest to it. What he saw froze his blood but he managed to let out a strangled scream of warning: 'Snake! Run! Run!'

The boys took one shocked look at the massive cobra whose brown coils stood out clearly against the green grass. Its hood was raised and it was gliding towards them in a slow, purposeful manner. With one accord, they turned and fled, running so fast that their legs were a blur, their breaths coming in painful gasps and their hearts pounding. Some precious minutes elapsed before they realized that their leader had not responded to their screams. They ran, shouting frenziedly, to his house to summon help.

In no time at all, the boys were back at the grove with Naren's agitated parents in tow, peering fearfully through the foliage and expecting to see their friend in the throes of death. What they saw, though, made them smile in relief but deepened the mystery all the more. Naren was sitting just as they had left him on the tussock of grass with his eyes shut. There was no sign of the massive cobra.

Naren's mother ran to him and hugged him fiercely. 'You are safe, my dear boy!' she exclaimed, tears running down her face. Naren opened his eyes and looked at the distressed group before him, a slight frown creasing his brow. 'What's the matter? I was just thinking.'

In later years, this amazing power of concentration was one of the most marked aspects of Vivekananda's personality. Not only did it enable him to master his subjects at school and thereafter, but also to concentrate on a thought or argument with single-minded focus until he had arrived at a solution.

Naren started his studies when he was six years old. His mother taught him the alphabets. Then he learned to read and write from a teacher who came home. He soon proved to have a photographic memory. He only had to look at a page once to know its contents by heart. When Naren was seven, he was sent to the Metropolitan Institution, a school in Kolkata started by the social reformer, Pandit Ishwar Chandra Vidyasagar. His exceptional intelligence and grasping power were immediately recognized by his teachers who marvelled at his ability to learn lessons so quickly and thoroughly.

This intelligent boy, though, was of such a restless temperament that he would talk to his friends and tell them stories even while the teacher was present in the classroom. Once the teacher, annoyed at the murmuring and general inattention among the boys, asked them to repeat the lesson just taught and to answer some questions based on it. None, except Naren, was able to do so. Clearly he had been able to focus equally on two things at the same time! Undeterred, the teacher asked who had been talking. Naren stood up and said, 'I must stand for it was I who was talking.' Then and throughout his life, Naren was a stickler for the truth irrespective of the consequences—a lesson his mother had imprinted on him at a very early age. However, Naren used a lot of his energy not so much in studying but in games and sports instead. He would eat his lunch as fast as he could so that he could be out in the playground with his other friends. Here too, he was a leader not the least for his ability to invent games of various kinds. There was never a dull moment with him around!

Interestingly, throughout his childhood, Naren surrounded himself with animals. Apart from their family cow with whom he would play for hours on end, he had a monkey, a goat, a peacock, some pigeons and a couple of guinea pigs. His fondness for animals continued throughout his life and during his final days, he had a dog called Bagha, a kid called Matru and several ducks, geese and sheep, all of whom he loved dearly.

In later years in school, Naren organized an amateur theatrical company. He took lessons in fencing, wrestling, rowing and other sports. He also tried his hand at cooking and discovered that he enjoyed it immensely. During his travels as Vivekananda, he would cook elaborate meals for his followers and friends. His liberal use of spices and chillies, however, made a lot of his foreigner friends choke and drink gallons of water while eating his food!

Although Naren's interest and curiosity in different activities was boundless, he would tire very quickly of his current pastime and cast about for a new one. On one occasion, he wanted to set up a heavy trapeze in the gymnasium in town. It was a difficult task, and Naren and his friends were visibly struggling with the equipment although none of the onlookers offered to help. An English sailor, who was one of the bystanders, eventually offered to assist the boys. He had just started helping them when the trapeze unaccountably swung out of their grasp, crashing down on the unfortunate sailor's head. He fell heavily to the floor, bleeding profusely from a gash on his head. The crowd and most of Naren's friends, fearing that the sailor was dead, took to their heels and ran away from the scene.

Naren now took charge of the situation. He tore a piece of cloth from his dhoti to make a rough bandage. With the help of some friends who had stayed behind, he bandaged the unconscious sailor's head, washed his face and attempted to revive him. To their relief, the sailor regained consciousness soon after. He was then escorted by them to a neighbouring schoolhouse. A doctor was summoned and Naren spent the rest of that week tending to the sailor's wounds and attending to his needs. Meanwhile, he managed to raise some money from among his friends and presented this to the sailor when the latter had recovered completely.

Another incident from Naren's childhood points to his impatience with superstition of all sorts—an aspect that remained unchanged throughout his life. A flowering tree in a neighbour's compound was one of Naren's favourite haunts. He would climb it, despite the owner's remonstrance, pluck the flowers and swing his legs from a branch with merry abandon until he finally somersaulted to the ground. The neighbour's irritation mounted until he devised what he thought was a foolproof plan. Summoning Naren's friends, he warned them that a ghost lived in that tree and it would break their necks if they disturbed its peace.

Accordingly, when Naren reached the compound for his usual spot of mischief, he was accosted by a set of terrified boys who begged him not to climb the tree. Naren's response was to swing himself up on to the lowest branch whereupon he proceeded to climb with his usual agility. The boys peered up at him, ashen-faced at the thought of what was to follow. When Naren had had his fill of climbing, he sat on a branch and shouted down to his friends, 'What fools you are to believe that story! Isn't my neck still there? If the story were true, don't you think my neck would have broken long before this?' Later, he would tell audiences around the world, 'Do not believe in a thing because you have read about it in a book. Do not believe in a thing because another man has said it was true ... Find out the truth for yourself. Reason it out. That is realization.'

Once when Naren was about eleven years old, a British warship entered the port of Kolkata. The event created a huge stir in the city and all were agog to see the vessel at close quarters. Naren's curiosity was at fever pitch, too, and he determined to visit the warship with his friends. Discovering that a pass from an important British official was a requisite, he filled in an application form and took it to the building where the official stayed. However, the doorkeeper refused to allow Naren entry because he thought the boy was too young.

When his protests fell on deaf ears, Naren stood aside observing the crowd. He noticed that everyone was heading towards a room on the first floor of the building. Suspecting the existence of another entrance, he strolled round to the rear of the building where he found a staircase that was unmanned. Overjoyed, he climbed the stairs to the first floor and took his place in the queue for the pass. The British official signed his application without question and Naren then left by the main entrance. The doorkeeper was stunned to see him emerge and asked him angrily how he had got in.

'Oh, don't you know I am a magician?' was Naren's cheeky reply.

Meanwhile, despite Naren's high-spirited mischief and wild games, he was still subjected to iron discipline at home by his father. Bisvanath had a unique manner of enforcing manners and courtesy. When Naren, on one occasion, argued impetuously with his mother and uttered some rude words, his father learned of it but did not rebuke his son directly. Instead, he wrote with charcoal on the door of Naren's room: 'Narendra today said to his mother . . .' and added the words that had been said. A shamefaced Naren, worried that his friends would read this message on his door, was forced to regret his hasty words and resolved never to use them in the future.

As Naren grew, his intellectual abilities became more and more apparent. His reading was varied and eclectic, ranging from newspapers that he devoured to books on history, and English and Bengali literature. In 1877, the Datta family moved to Raipur for two years. Here, Naren stopped going to school but was encouraged by his father to meet scholars and discuss topics with them that were considered too intellectual and abstruse for children of his age but which were actually well within Naren's levels of comprehension.

In 1879, when the family returned to Kolkata, Naren had to squeeze in all the work he had missed into one year. However, he sailed through his examinations and passed them in the first division—a rare academic honour. By now, he had acquired an unusual method of reading a book and understanding its content. He could understand without reading every line of the book. He remarked later, 'I would read the first and last lines of a paragraph and grasp its meaning. Later I found that I could understand the subject matter by reading only the first and last lines of a page. Afterwards I could follow the whole trend of a writer's argument by merely reading a few lines, though the author himself tried to explain the subject in five or more pages.' Undoubtedly, he was a voracious reader but his unique manner of mastering a book's content also serves to highlight the breadth of his intellectual genius.

Who was 'Vidyasagar'?

Ishwar Chandra Bandopadhyaya (1820–1891) was an eminent scholar and social reformer of 19th century Bengal. He was born at a time when the doors to English education were being thrown open to Indians. Through this, India was brought into close contact with Western culture, some of whose aspects she began to imbibe. Ishwar Chandra was to play a significant role in giving shape to this new culture that was being born. In later years, he received the title 'Vidyasagar' (ocean of learning/knowledge) from the Calcutta Sanskrit College due to his excellent performance in Sanskrit studies and philosophy.

Vidyasagar championed the cause of women in India, particularly in Bengal. He introduced the practice of widow remarriage in Hindu society, and proposed and pushed through the Widow Remarriage Act XV of 1856 in India.

3 🕉 'Have You Seen God?'

As time wore on and Naren crossed the line from boyhood to adulthood, books remained his passion and so did music. He possessed an extremely melodious voice and was often invited to sing at congregational prayers and other gatherings. Naren could play several instruments as well and excelled in a wide range of devotional songs. Music, especially classical music in which he had been trained, would often transport him to another world. However, what he enjoyed above everything else, were intellectual discussions and arguments. Few people could match his skills in this field.

In 1879, Naren joined the Presidency College of Calcutta for higher studies. However, after a year, he left and joined the General Assembly's Institution, which was founded by the Scottish General Missionary Board and later became known as the Scottish Church College. Here too, Naren impressed his professors, particularly his principal, Professor William Hastie, with his intelligence and ability to comprehend complex subjects with perfect ease. Professor Hastie once remarked, 'Narendra is a real genius. I have travelled far and wide, but have not yet come across a lad of his talents and possibilities even among the philosophical students in the German universities. He is bound to make his mark in life.'

It was Hastie, also a professor of English literature, who first told Naren about Sri Ramakrishna Paramahansa, the man who later became Naren's spiritual mentor and played a crucial role in his life. While teaching William Wordsworth's poem, The *Excursion*, to his class, Professor Hastie explained that the trance-like state of mind into which the poet was transported could, in fact, be a real experience and not just a flight of poetic fancy. He noted, however, that this state could not be attained without the utmost inner purity, which was extremely rare. Hastie then remarked that he had seen only one person who had experienced that blessed state of mind and he was Ramakrishna Paramahansa of Dakshineswar. The boys would understand it if they went there and saw him for themselves.

At the time, Naren was studying Western logic and philosophy. He had studied and assimilated the works of the renowned English philosophers—David Hume, Herbert Spencer and John Stuart Mill. However, he was now beginning to be consumed by a yearning for God; to know if he existed at all and if anyone had ever seen him. At the same time, his study of Western rationalist philosophy filled his mind with doubts and forced him to take a critical look at this quest. He could neither dismiss the force of these rational arguments nor deny his own desperate yearning.

Hastie's statement about Ramakrishna Paramahansa intrigued Naren greatly. His curiosity aroused, he determined to visit Dakshineswar to meet this saint. Yet it would take some time for Naren and Sri Ramakrishna to meet.

Meanwhile, like many other youths of his age, Naren had joined the Brahmo Samaj, an important socio-religious movement founded by Raja Rammohan Roy that had captured the imagination of the educated youths of Bengal. At the time, Hinduism was marked by an extremely rigid and oppressive caste structure, along with the dominance of the priests who largely perpetuated their own selfish interests. Meaningless rituals and rites abounded in the name of which the masses were exploited. Influenced by Western culture, the Brahma Samaj upheld the supremacy of reason and preached against the unthinking acceptance of scriptural authority. It was also a religious movement with belief in one God.

For a while, the congregational prayers and devotional songs of the Brahmo Samaj satisfied Naren, who felt the appeal of its progressive ideas. However, the attraction began to wane when he realized that these gatherings did not give him any real spiritual experience. Accordingly, one day, he went up to Devendranath Tagore, one of the leaders of the Brahmo Samaj, and asked him without any preamble, 'Sir, have you seen God?'

Devendranath Tagore thoughtfully studied the young man before remarking, 'My boy, you have the eyes of a *yogi*. You should practice meditation.' This reply left Naren extremely disappointed as his question had not been answered. He now became even more restless and approached several other religious figures with the same query in the hope of finding guidance. Invariably, the answer was 'no'.

At about this time, Naren received a marriage proposal. A wealthy man offered his daughter's hand to Naren and promised to pay for his expenses for higher studies in England so that he could eventually join the coveted Indian Civil Service. Naren declined this and several other proposals which followed despite his father's insistence.

It so happened that one of Naren's relatives, Ramachandra Datta, who was an ardent devotee of Sri Ramakrishna, learned of Naren's unwillingness to marry and presumed it was because of his desire to lead a spiritual life. He told Naren, 'If you really want to cultivate spirituality, then visit Ramakrishna at Dakshineswar.' This was the second time that Naren had heard this saint's name.

He finally got an opportunity to meet Ramakrishna at the house of Surendranath Mitra, one of Sri Ramakrishna's devotees, who had invited Naren one evening to sing. This was in the year 1881 and the meeting proved to be one of the most important events of Naren's life which would transform its course completely.

It is necessary to have some idea about Ramakrishna Paramahansa before describing the effect he had on Naren's life. Sri Ramakrishna was born on 18 February 1836 to a poor brahmana couple in a village called Kamarpukur in the Hooghly district of Bengal. He was given the name Gadadhar Chattopadhyaya. When their father died, Gadadhar's elder brother, Ramkumar, moved to Kolkata and opened a school there in 1850. Gadadhar went to live with him two years later, but did not show the slightest interest in studies or a formal education of any kind. He wanted to focus on realizing God but this quest was so intense that he fell ill and had to move back to Kamarpukur.

At this point, Gadadhar's family persuaded him to marry a very young girl, Saradamani, or Sarada Devi, in May 1859. At that time, she was a little over six years old. She continued to live with her parents after the marriage while Gadadhar returned to Kolkata. Meanwhile, at Dakshineswar, four miles north of Kolkata on the east bank of the river Ganga, Rani Rasmani, a rich widow from a lower caste, had built a magnificent Kali temple. But no brahmana would accept the post of a priest there. Gadadhar's brother, Ramkumar, eventually agreed to take on this position despite the disapproval of almost everyone, including Gadadhar himself.

Later, when Ramkumar grew old and could no longer perform his duties, Gadadhar took over from him for he had completely reversed his ideas on caste by then. He now lived in Dakshineswar as priest to the deity, Kali. At the same time, he was already becoming known for going into sudden trances, and singing and dancing in that state. He would also have many conversations with Kali whose presence he could feel and who apparently resolved all his doubts. People thought Gadadhar was either mad or divinely inspired and many came to see him out of curiosity or to seek his blessings.

Gadadhar was now seized by a sudden desire to experience various religious faiths. Accordingly, he was freed from his duties at the temple while he practised, in turn, the path of tantra, Vaishnava bhakti, the path of Vedanta, the path of Islam and then the path of Christianity. Thereafter, he followed the path of the Buddha, the Jaina tirthankaras and the Sikh gurus. Incidentally, it was a wandering monk, Totapuri, under whom he practised Vedanta, who gave him the name 'Ramakrishna' and initiated him into *sanyasa*.

At the end of this period of religious experimentation, Sri Ramakrishna concluded that all faiths lead to the same goal—the realization of God—and this knowledge made man free. Naren, as Vivekananda, would later share this realization with a world that was rent by religious hatred. Meanwhile, Sarada Devi arrived at Dakshineswar to take care of her husband and assist him on his spiritual journey. Sri Ramakrishna saw her as another form of Kali or the divine mother.

It was at around this time that Sri Ramakrishna heard Naren sing at Surendranath Mitra's house and immediately recognized his innate greatness and foresaw his future path. He asked Naren to visit him at Dakshineswar. Naren, who felt an inexplicable attraction towards this man, agreed to do so. However, their first meeting at Dakshineswar proved to be profoundly unsettling for Naren. Sri Ramakrishna was normal in front of everyone but eventually took Naren into a room and behaved in a manner that made Naren wonder whether he was actually a great mystic saint or someone who was completely mad.

Naren later recalled, 'I thought he (Sri Ramakrishna) might perhaps give me some instructions in private. But what he said and did was beyond imagination. He suddenly caught hold of my hand and shed profuse tears of joy. Addressing me affectionately like one already familiar, he said: "Is it proper that you should come so late? Should you not have once thought how I was waiting for you?" ... The next moment he stood before me with folded palms and said, "I know, my lord, you are that ancient Rishi Nara, a part of Narayana, who has incarnated himself this time, to remove the miseries and sufferings of humanity."'

Naren was flabbergasted not just by these words but also by Sri Ramakrishna's subsequent action of feeding him sweets with his own hands, begging him to return to Dakshineswar as soon as he could. However, when they emerged from the room, the saint was again completely normal and Naren, who was observing him closely, could find no trace of madness in his behaviour or conversation. Sri Ramakrishna's subsequent remarks, though, made an impression on Naren's agitated mind. He said, 'God can be seen and spoken with just as I am seeing you and speaking with you; but who wants to do so? ... If any one is in truth equally anxious to see Him and calls on Him with a longing heart, he certainly reveals Himself to him.' Naren instinctively felt that these words were not born of Sri Ramakrishna's imagination but stemmed from knowledge, which had come to him because he had renounced everything for the sake of God. He was impressed by this saint despite his strange behaviour and resolved to visit him again.

Naren's second visit to Dakshineswar was, however, almost a month later. This time, he was even more alarmed by Sri Ramakrishna's behaviour. Naren had gone directly to the saint's room and saw him sitting alone on the bedstead. He called out joyfully to Naren, made him sit down and then placed his right foot on Naren's body. Naren immediately had what he later describes as a 'wonderful experience'. The room along with its walls appeared to be whirling and receding into a void, and so was he along with the entire universe. Naren was suddenly overcome by fear and cried, 'Ah! What is it you have done to me? I have my parents, you know.'

Sri Ramakrishna laughed at Naren's words, touched his chest and said, 'Let it then cease now. It need not be done all at once. It will come to pass in course of time.' Everything returned to normal at once but Naren was left feeling extremely disturbed. He wondered whether he had been hypnotized but had a feeling that the truth was more complex than that. Right from his boyhood, Naren had never accepted any conclusion unless it had been arrived at after proper observation, investigation and reasoning. He knew he could not be fooled, tricked or influenced very easily. The shock that he received on that day agitated his mind but also made him more determined to understand the nature and power of this mysterious saint who seemed to know more about him than he did himself.

The Brahmo Samaj

With the introduction of the British system of education in India following the colonization of the country, many drawbacks of Indian society came into sharp focus, resulting in the emergence of various reform movements which sought to address the problem. The Brahmo Samaj was one of these. The it was an influential socio-religious reform movement of the nineteenth century. It aimed at the emancipation of women, the abolition of child marriage and the spread of mass education. Raja Rammohan Roy, the founder of the movement, had a wide knowledge of varied religious scriptures and realized the importance of the Western rational method for solving the diverse problems of Indian society. He exhorted his followers to abandon the rituals, image worship and priest-craft of orthodox Hinduism, and played a prominent role in the introduction of English education in the country. Keshab Chandra Sen (1838–1884), a Bengali religious preacher and social reformer, was a leading member of the Brahmo Samaj but later founded his own breakaway Brahmo Samaj of India in 1866.

4   Searching for the Divine

It took Naren four years to thoroughly comprehend Sri Ramakrishna's nature and appreciate the mystic connection that clearly existed between them. He realized that what had initially appeared to him as the saint's madness was simply the latter's intoxication with God coupled with his childlike simplicity. That he had a deep love for Naren was also very clear; it was expressed on a number of occasions and, more often than not, would catch Naren by surprise and completely overwhelm him by its intensity.

On one occasion, when Sri Ramakrishna had not seen Naren for several days, he decided to visit the latter at his home in Kolkata. On arriving there, he was told that Naren was studying in his room upstairs which was a kind of attic that could only be reached by a steep staircase. Undeterred, Sri Ramakrishna climbed the stairs with great difficulty and burst into Naren's room. He hugged the startled Naren, wept for joy and then immediately went into a trance.

Naren's prolonged absence from Dakshineswar on another occasion prompted the saint to undertake the arduous journey to Kolkata again. Being a Sunday, he guessed rightly that Naren would be singing at the congregational prayer meeting of the Brahmo Samaj. Accordingly, he astonished everyone, particularly Naren, by arriving at the prayer venue and going into a trance on seeing his protégé. No one there greeted him or made the slightest effort to make him feel welcome. In fact, someone even went to the extent of switching off the lights in the prayer hall, plunging the situation into further chaos.

Naren, though a trifle annoyed at the saint's unannounced arrival, was nevertheless furious at this insult to him. He knew that the inner politics of the Brahmo Samaj was responsible for this: some members felt that their elder leaders like Keshab Chandra Sen had grown closer to Sri Ramakrishna and had, therefore, strayed from their original ideals. Naren sprang to his feet, stumbled over to Sri Ramakrishna in the darkness, managed to get him into a carriage and escorted him back to Dakshineswar. Hurt beyond belief at the callous treatment meted out to the saint, Naren scolded him for the foolhardy trip to Kolkata on his account. Naren's angry words, however, had no effect on Sri Ramakrishna who bore a satisfied smile on his face because he was with Naren once more. Frustrated, Naren cried, 'Why do you do such things?'

The saint's answer was simple: 'Because I can't help it.'

This was also the period when Naren began to understand himself and his potential more thoroughly. Physically, he was of medium stature with a strong but rather thickset figure. His big eyes, however, gave an immediate glimpse of his mental prowess. Clear and luminous, they shone with intelligence and passion, and also mirrored his restlessness and disquiet. They often twinkled with merriment as well for Naren had a good sense of humour just like his mentor.

Although deeply moved by Sri Ramakrishna's love for him, Naren initially regarded the saint's trances and visions as mere 'hallucinations' and did not hesitate to tell him so. Sri Ramakrishna would listen attentively but sometimes grow disturbed. He would then confess his fears to the figure of Kali, and she would apparently reassure him with predictions like 'Let him say what he likes. He will come round one day.' Naren would promptly reject these assurances and cite Western logic in support of his disbelieving stance.

On one occasion, the saint asked Naren, 'When you do not accept most of what I say, then why do you come here?' Naren's answer was simple, 'I come here to see you,' he said, 'and not to listen to you.' The saint was not unduly troubled by this answer because he knew that Naren would eventually come round.

And so, the meetings at Dakshineswar went on. Naren, along with the disciples and followers of Sri Ramakrishna would listen to the saint's discourse and debate questions of spirituality with much enthusiasm. Several eminent persons such as Keshab Chandra Sen and Girish Chandra Ghosh (a dramatist and poet), as well as hundreds of ordinary men and women of different faiths and social standings, attended these gatherings. Sri Ramakrishna would tell them that all religions lead to the same truth that is God; a thought that Naren would later build upon and communicate to the world while preaching against religious hatred and rivalries. Incidentally, these sessions were also marked with great humour because Sri Ramakrishna believed that 'God-consciousness' need not exclude fun and laughter. More often than not, Naren would be persuaded to sing and he would entrance everyone with his beautiful renditions of devotional songs.

Naren, however, continued to be brutally honest with Sri Ramakrishna and would speak his mind frankly even if it went against what the saint said and angered his followers. One day, Naren told Sri Ramakrishna that he had eaten what was considered forbidden food at a hotel. The saint could now choose to shun his touch or even his presence. However, Sri Ramakrishna made an exception in Naren's case as the latter's mind was always fixed on the spiritual.

It was during one of the discussions at Dakshineswar that Naren learned the essence of Sri Ramakrishna's teachings—that the love of God meant putting oneself in the service of others and, therefore, the aim of bhakti or devotion was not to seek one's own salvation but to do service to mankind in whom God resided. Thus, man could not talk in terms of showing compassion to others—as he was an insignificant creature in the scheme of things—but should only be of service to others.

Naren was astounded by this new interpretation of bhakti, one that was not a dry, austere philosophy but a faith that connected men to each other in a pure bond.

Thus, one did not have to renounce the world altogether to seek the divine but could serve mankind instead in whom God was manifested. More importantly, if each person was a part of God, then no one could consider himself superior to the other, and there would be no room for anger, hatred or arrogance of any kind. 'If the divine Lord ever grants me an opportunity,' Naren declared, 'I'll proclaim everywhere in the world this wonderful truth I have heard today. I will preach this truth to the learned and the ignorant, to the rich and the poor, to the Brahmana and the Chandala.' His desire was to come true when, as Vivekananda, he would communicate this message of his master to the world.

However, it is hard to pinpoint the exact moment when Naren accepted Sri Ramakrishna as his mentor or guru. Perhaps it was the saint's implicit faith in and love for him that led Naren from doubt to certainty. It could also be that he alone spoke of God with certainty when all other religious figures, as well as the leaders of the Brahmo Samaj, had failed to aid Naren's spiritual quest. That the saint encouraged Naren in his independent thinking and did not force any conclusions upon him was perhaps another strong binding factor between the two.

It was at this time, though, that the Datta family was plunged into tragedy. On 13 February 1884 when Naren was just twenty-one, his father, Bisvanath, died of heart failure. Naren was with a friend when the news was brought to him and the ground momentarily disappeared from beneath his feet. Stunned and grief-stricken, he had hardly begun to mourn the loss of his beloved father when fresh disasters struck the family. Bisvanath, always reckless in scattering his largesse, had left virtually no money behind for his family to sustain itself. Moreover, some relatives and friends whom Bisvanath had trusted, had borrowed money in his name and squandered it, accumulating a string of debts that the creditors were now intent on recovering. Around the same time, an aunt, who was living with her family under the Dattas' roof and had long been supported by Bisvanath, claimed that this ancestral house was legally hers, and filed a lawsuit to take possession of it.

Naren had enrolled himself for a degree in law after his graduation but had to now abandon his studies as, being the eldest son, the responsibility of the family fell upon his shoulders. It was an exceedingly traumatic time for the Dattas as even two meals a day were difficult to come by. Naren, meanwhile, traversed the streets of Kolkata all day, desperately seeking a job, but only met with refusals. Returning home hungry and tired in the evening, he would pretend to have eaten something outside so that others could eat his share of food. On the other hand, if he was at a friend's house and was offered a meal, he would say that he had already eaten at home for he could not bear to eat good food while his family went hungry.

As time wore on, Naren managed to find some work, once in a solicitor's office and, on another occasion, at Ishwar Chandra Vidyasagar's school, but it was a fragile existence for he barely made enough money to cover the daily expenses. He grew frustrated and cynical with the lack of sympathy around him. He later remarked, 'I noticed that those who only a few days ago would have been proud to help me in any way, now turned their face against me, though they had enough and to spare. Seeing all this, the world sometimes seemed to me to be the handiwork of the devil.' In retrospect, though, Naren's personal experience of privation and hunger equipped him to deal with the weak, the poor and the destitute in later years with sympathy and understanding, and gave him the strength to overcome pain and suffering of all kinds.

Naren's self-respect prevented him from asking his friends for help. Only one of them came to know about his desperate situation and would send money to Naren's mother at intervals but anonymously. Naren was immensely grateful for this help but began to lose faith in the existence of a loving, merciful God. In fact, whenever he heard any of his friends sing a devotional song, he would command them to stop.

Naren's feelings of bitterness were known to Sri Ramakrishna who was deeply troubled by the young man's state. However, when Naren told him, 'I am now studying the views of atheists,' he gently remarked, 'There are two doctrines: the existence and the non-existence of God. Why don't you accept the first?' However, Naren would not be swayed. His father's death and his dealings with greedy, unscrupulous people thereafter made him feel that God did not exist and that, even if he did, he was certainly not merciful. Moreover, he did not bother to hide his views and, before long, was labelled as not just an atheist but also one who had got into drinking and other bad ways.

Furious and resentful at these false accusations, and worried about their effect on his mother and his mentor, Naren perversely declared that he was not scared of anybody, had no objection to drinking and would even do so if he was convinced that it would make him feel happy for a moment. The rumours reached Dakshineswar in due course but Sri Ramakrishna dismissed them outright. His faith in Naren remained unchanged.

Unable to bear the sufferings of his family any longer, Naren requested Sri Ramakrishna to intercede with the divine mother, Kali, on his behalf to put an end to his misery. However, the saint informed Naren that he had never made any personal request to the goddess, either for himself or for anyone else, and that he should, therefore, appeal to her himself. Accordingly, Naren went and stood before the image of Kali but suddenly passed into a consciousness where there were no distinctions and everything seemed to be permeated with God.

He emerged a while later with a look of utter bliss on his face. 'Did you appeal to the Divine Mother?' asked Sri Ramakrishna.

'Oh, I forgot,' Naren answered.

'Then go again.'

Naren went before the idol twice more and felt the same consciousness of God each time. He completely forgot to ask his question. This experience affected Naren profoundly on different levels. His feeling for the sufferings of others grew from that consciousness and he would eventually dedicate his life to removing them. Meanwhile, Naren's family strove to understand his growing preoccupation with religion and the resultant remoteness. Despite his spending long hours at Dakshineswar, they did not rebuke him. Perhaps they already had an inkling that he belonged to the world rather than to them.

The Bhakti Movement
The Bhakti movement began in south India with the Vaishnava Alvars (6th–9th century CE) and Shaiva Nayanars (5th–10th century CE), who popularized bhakti or loving devotion to God through poetry and other means. The movement later spread to the north. The Bhakti movement taught that people should cast aside ritual and caste, and simply express their overwhelming love for God. It was an important component of many branches of Hinduism and was defined differently by various sects. Some of the leading Bhakti saints of the north were Ravidas, Surdas, Meera Bai and Kabir. Karaikkal Ammaiyar and Andal were two famous women Bhakti saints of the south.

5 🙂 A Death and a Family

Tragedy loomed large again for Naren towards the end of 1885. Sri Ramakrishna, who had been troubled by a sore throat for some months, was finally diagnosed with throat cancer. He was placed under the care of Dr Mahendra Lal Sarkar, a renowned homoeopath of Kolkata. Dakshineswar was, however, quite some distance from Kolkata where all his young disciples, including Naren, lived. Besides, it did not have the required medical or nursing facilities that his condition required. Accordingly, Sri Ramakrishna was moved to Kolkata. He stayed at the house of one of his devotees, Balaram Bose, for a while, then in a rented house at Shyampukur and, later, from 11 December 1885, at a spacious garden-house at Cossipore or Kasipur.

Here, his young disciples, headed by Naren, nursed him night and day, hoping that the dreaded disease would somehow loosen its hold on him and that he would make a full recovery. Sarada Devi also moved into the house at Cossipore to take care of her ailing husband. This was a fairly formidable task for her as she was an exceptionally shy person but she tried her best to adjust to a household that was full of men, mostly strangers to her.

Sri Ramakrishna, meanwhile, continued with his routine activities despite being in considerable pain. While trying to prepare his disciples for a life of renunciation, he made sure that the daily spiritual gatherings and debates took place unabated, marked by the same singing interludes and merriment as at Dakshineswar. His disciples, students and householders among them, abandoned their worldly concerns and completely devoted themselves to his care, Naren most of all.

Naren's absences from home became more and more frequent as Sri Ramakrishna's illness took a turn for the worse. His brother, Bhupendranath's, biography tells us that their mother was very upset by this and determined to bring Naren back home. Accordingly, she took the six-year-old Bhupendranath along with her to the house at Cossipore. Both were promptly ushered into the saint's presence. Sri Ramakrishna took one look at Naren's mother and told her to take Naren back with her. He said that he had already told Naren to look after his widowed mother and young brother instead of renouncing them. Consequently, a reluctant and sullen Naren accompanied his mother and brother on their way home, but got off the carriage midway on some pretext and went back to his beloved guru. Nothing in the world, not even pressing family concerns, could keep him away from Cossipore now.

In fact, Naren's mother was unaware that her son's desire to renounce the world had already been thwarted once before by Sri Ramakrishna. In the troubled days following his father's death, Naren had once travelled from Kolkata to Dakshineswar to inform his mentor of his decision to renounce the world, that too on a particular date. Although Sri Ramakrishna was aware that this was exactly what Naren would do one day, he dissuaded him from taking this step then, saying, 'Know that you have come to the world for Mother's work: you can never live a worldly life. But remain in your family for my sake as long as I live.' The wording of his plea is curious. Perhaps Sri Ramakrishna feared that Naren might leave him too if he gave up the world, a separation that he could not have borne.

Meanwhile, an unusual bond of friendship was developing between the physician, Dr Sarkar, and Sri Ramakrishna. The former, undemonstrative by nature, grew to revere his patient and his affection was all the more poignant as he knew the saint was dying. Sri Ramakrishna, too, looked forward to the daily exchange of banter and heated arguments with Dr Sarkar. On one occasion, Girish Chandra Ghosh asked the doctor, 'You have already spent three or four hours here. What about your patients?'

Dr Sarkar answered with a rueful smile, 'Well, my practice and patients! I shall lose everything on account of your *paramahansa*!'

Speaking his mind in a forthright manner was one of the doctor's traits and he challenged Sri Ramakrishna's assertions on a number of occasions. In this regard, he resembled Naren who continued to argue with the saint despite spending every hour caring for him with tenderness and love, having even given up his final law examination for this.

The saint once remarked, 'Some people call me God.' Naren promptly replied, 'Let a thousand people call you God, but I shall certainly not call you God as long as I do not know it to be true.'

It was around this time that while meditating one evening, Naren suddenly entered an exalted state and lost all consciousness of his body except for his head. He then passed into a deep trance from which he emerged only hours later. Sri Ramakrishna stopped him from thinking about this ultimate bliss by telling him, 'You have work to do.' He later remarked to his other disciples that the time would come 'when Naren will shake the world to its foundations.'

The twelve other disciples, meanwhile, had formed a close bond between themselves but they all looked upon Naren with awe even though some of them were about his age. His intellect, dynamism and determination completely impressed them. He could, at times, be aloof or impatient while, at others, incredibly tender. They feared yet respected his forthright manner and frank demeanour, and this was nowhere more evident than in his harsh criticism of their illogical habit of seeing the supernatural even in natural things.

Sri Ramakrishna's illness was a case in point. Some of the disciples believed that his ailment had a divine purpose and when this end had been served, he would be healthy again. Some others felt that he had taken the sins of others upon himself and this had taken the form of cancer. Naren was brutally honest with them and argued that Sri Ramakrishna's body, like all other human bodies, was naturally subject to disease and death. He ridiculed their supernatural explanations and repeatedly reminded them of one of Sri Ramakrishna's favourite sayings: 'You should be a devotee, it is true, but why should you, therefore, be a fool?'

A few days before his death, Sri Ramakrishna summoned Naren to his bedside and wrote on a piece of paper, 'Naren will teach others', implying that he would be in charge of the other disciples after the saint's death.

'I won't do any such thing,' Naren declared.

'Your very bones will do it,' whispered Sri Ramakrishna.

This was a prophetic statement. Time would show Naren fulfilling this task in an exemplary way. He would be worshipped in India for his teachings and would also touch innumerable hearts in the West through them. That was the future, however. Meanwhile, in the present, Sri Ramakrishna, after a brave battle with cancer, finally succumbed to it and passed away on 16 August 1886. His wife, Sarada Devi, was to follow him thirty-four years later on 21 July 1920. After her husband's death, however, she moved to the house of Balaram Bose. Then she shifted to Vrindavan for a year, returned briefly to Kolkata and finally settled down in Kamarpukur. She lived a life of loneliness and poverty. Much later, though, one of the monks, Swami Saradananda, would devote himself to her care.

Following his mentor's death, the responsibility of another family—that of Sri Ramakrishna's disciples—now fell on Naren's shoulders. He was only twenty-four years of age at the time but was equal to this onerous task. A house in Baranagore in the suburbs of Kolkata (which was even rumoured to be haunted!) was rented for the disciples with the help of Surendranath Mitra, Sri Ramakrishna's dedicated follower, who paid the rent and provided the monks with other necessities. The Baranagore Math, as this new monastery was called, thus became the first headquarters of the monks of the Ramakrishna Order. At its centre was the shrine room where the ashes of Sri Ramakrishna were kept in a vessel and worshipped daily. Incidentally, it remained the monks' headquarters from 1886 till 1992 when it shifted to Alambazar near Dakshineswar, which continued to function as the headquarters till 1897. The Belur Math became their final headquarters in 1898.

Most of the twelve disciples of Sri Ramakrishna came from Hindu middle-class families. Some had parents and children, and all had responsibilities and obligations of one sort or the other. Naren's dilemma was no less. Not only did he have to make some arrangement for his family's upkeep but he also had to attend to the lawsuit that his aunt had earlier filed against his family. He later recalled, 'I had to stand between my two worlds. On the one hand, I would have to see my mother and brothers starve unto death; on the other, I had believed that this man's (Sri Ramakrishna's) ideas were for the good of India and the world, and had to be preached and worked out.' His joy at embracing a life of spirituality was tempered by sorrow for the family he was leaving behind.

Nevertheless, pushing aside their individual concerns, the young disciples of Sri Ramakrishna conducted a ceremony called *viraja* at Baranagore around the end of 1886 during which they took the two vows of chastity and poverty, and adopted the ochre robe. On formally entering monastic life, they gave themselves new names by which they were to be known thereafter, each to be preceded by the word 'Swami'. For example, Rakhal and Sharat called themselves Swami Brahmananda and Swami Saradananda, respectively. By now, there were fifteen of them in all as some more had joined their order over time.

Naren alone did not give himself any particular monastic name. Later, during his wanderings in India, he sometimes called himself Swami Vividishananda or Satchidananda but right then, he continued to use his original name. Naren did not live at the Baranagore Math all the time as most of his brother-monks did. During the day, he would usually be at home attending to matters pertaining to the lawsuit and other issues concerning his family. However, he would return to Baranagore in the evening. Deeply conscious of the fact that Sri Ramakrishna had entrusted 'the boys' to his care, he took this responsibility as seriously as he did all others that fell to his lot.

The atmosphere at the Baranagore Math was charged with a strong spirituality as well as by a deep bond of togetherness. Naren was eager that his family of monks open their minds to the world around them, and know both its past and present. Therefore, drawing from his vast repertoire of readings and knowledge, he started teaching them the history of civilization. At the same time, he introduced them to philosophical ideas from different parts of the world. Apart from the Sanskrit texts of Indian philosophy, the monks were to study Greek philosophy, and thinkers like John Locke, David Hume, John Stuart Mill and Herbert Spencer among others. They were even to study the fundamentals of physical sciences.

Naren was an inspired and brilliant teacher, himself seeking to learn all the time. As a visionary, he was always challenging the monks with new thoughts and ideas (that not all of them quite understood) and emphasizing the importance of reason and logic above all else. Naren was, however, a hard taskmaster. For instance, he insisted that the monks study Panini's *Ashtadhyayi* or rules of grammar in order to comprehend the Sanskrit texts more thoroughly. Not all his brother-monks reacted with equal enthusiasm to this new intellectual exercise that he was putting them through. Some of them were quite content with their meditation and recitation of the varied names of God. However, all of them were fascinated with Naren's description of the world and of the evolution of philosophy.

At the same time, Naren kept a vigilant eye out for any evidence of illogical beliefs. Once a member of the monastery pretended to be suffering greatly on account of his separation from God and said, 'Ah! Please get me a knife. I have no more use for this life.'

Naren promptly responded, 'It is there. Stretch out your hand and take it.'

Everyone around was reduced to laughter, including Naren and the monk himself, but despite the merriment, Naren's intent was clear to all. Their leader, who seemed to be surrounded now with an aura of radiance and tenderness, would not brook any kind of irrational thought or unfounded belief.

Naren's ochre robes, in fact, seemed to reflect the luminosity of his face. However, the spiritual energy he exuded was probably not completely his own but derived also from that of his mentor. Just before his death, Sri Ramakrishna had called Naren to him and looking deeply into his eyes had passed into a trance. Naren suddenly felt as if an electric charge was passing through his body. Emerging from the trance, Sri Ramakrishna burst into tears saying, 'Oh, Naren, today I have given you my all and have become a *faqir*, a penniless beggar.' Naren hardly ever talked about this event thereafter, but would later remark that, 'There is a force behind me greater than man, or god, or devil.' Whether he really accepted that energies could be transferred thus is uncertain but the young monk definitely believed in the transforming energy of love flowing from one person to another—and he was its greatest practitioner throughout his life.

Some interesting facts about the Ramakrishna Order

With the establishment of the Belur Math in 1899, the management of the Ramakrishna Order was turned over by Swami Vivekananda to a board of trustees comprising some of its monastic members. This system of management continues even now. Today the Ramakrishna Math is administered by a board of trustees, consisting of senior monks of the Order, chosen by a process of nomination-cum-election. Currently, the Ramakrishna Math and Mission has 171 centres all over the world.

Several lay people have also made valuable contributions to the Ramakrishna Order. One of them was Surendranath Mitra, who provided financial assistance. Ironically, his name is hardly known today even to those who worship Sri Ramakrishna. At the time, though, Naren was very vocal in his gratitude to him and publicly acknowledged his crucial help. There is another irony in Mitra's role. Sri Ramakrishna had always denounced 'gold' or money and had advised his followers to stay away from it. However, it was Mitra's 'gold' that enabled the saint's disciples to establish their order.

Incidentally, the value of money in those times was vastly different from that of today. For instance, for the first few months, Mitra contributed thirty rupees a month to the Math. As new members joined it, he doubled his contribution to sixty rupees and later increased it to a hundred rupees. The monthly rent for the house was eleven rupees. The cook was paid six rupees a month and the rest was spent on food!

6 🖼 The Travelling Saint

After a point, Naren began to feel somewhat stifled and restricted at Baranagore. He wanted to travel around the country and experience its vastness and complexities. Although he was still technically responsible for his brother-monks, life at the Math had taken on a routine, undisturbed even during Naren's rare absences. There was another worry off his mind now: the lawsuit that Naren's aunt had slapped on his family had been settled in favour of the Dattas. However, the litigation costs had left the family financially worse off than before. Yet, in some strange, unfathomable way, there was always just enough to keep them going, to keep body and soul together.

Naren, therefore, was now in a position to take some time out for himself. Accordingly, in 1888, on a date that remains uncertain, he left Baranagore for Varanasi. His choice of destination was guided by two reasons: one, this was considered one of the holiest places in the country and two, this was also where his grandfather, Durgaprasad, had gone when he had abandoned his family for a life of spirituality. However, Naren stayed only very briefly at Varanasi because he was anxious about his brother-monks. He, therefore, returned to Baranagore for a few months to discharge his responsibilities as before.

It was only thereafter that Naren began his long series of journeys in the country which spanned the years 1888 to 1893. Unfortunately, most of the dates as well as the actual sequence of his travels are not always known to us because Naren himself was rather casual about recording them. Some of the people that he met and stayed with during this period kept a record of his conversations and other relevant details but, again, not all of them are specific about the date, time and place of their occurrence.

During his travels, Naren influenced the lives of a varied number of people ranging from highly-educated persons like lawyers and doctors to those who were illiterate and poor, as also those of different religions. This sannyasin who spoke English with remarkable fluency was initially an object of curiosity but his words touched all whom he addressed. None who met Naren could ever forget the young monk with the powerful personality. For instance, his host at Trivandrum, K. Sundararama Iyer, recollected, '... during all the time he (Naren) stayed, he took captive every heart within the home. To everyone of us he was all sweetness, all tenderness, all grace ... When he left, it seemed for a while as if the light had gone out of our home.'

Naren's days as a wandering monk marked his use of new names. Thus, he called himself Swami Vividishananda or Swami Satchidananda at different points mainly to disguise his identity so that his brother-monks, who were feeling anchorless without him, would not attempt to track him down. A couple of them did, however, manage to track him to Delhi by following the trail of 'an English-speaking sadhu, Swami Vividishananda'. Although Naren was overjoyed to see them, he sternly forbade them from following him again. Naren wished to be alone with his thoughts and experiences. Having been beset with responsibilities and varied concerns all his life, it was small wonder that he now craved solitude!

During his travels, Naren often traversed long distances on foot or by train (if someone was obliging enough to buy him a ticket for his next destination). He sometimes travelled by bullock cart as well. He carried no money with him for he had taken a vow of poverty when he became a monk. When he left Baranagore, he had equipped himself with the bare necessities: a long staff, a monk's water jug, a change of ochre robes, a rough blanket with which to cover himself, and a copy each of the Bhagavadgita and *The Imitation of Christ* by the medieval monk, Thomas à Kempis. These were his only possessions.

Varanasi was Naren's first choice of destination again when he left Baranagore in 1888. Here, he had an unusual experience that taught him an important lesson. Closely pursued by a troop of monkeys one day, the young monk was running as fast as he could when a passing monk exclaimed, 'Don't run! Stand and face the brutes.' Naren stopped, turned around and looked defiantly at the monkeys who then quickly disappeared. He would later use this experience to teach people to confront their problems rather than run away from them.

From Varanasi, Naren went to Ayodhya, Lucknow, Agra, Vrindavan, Hathras, Haridwar and Rishikesh. It was at Hathras that he made his first monastic disciple under very unusual circumstances. It was sometime in 1888, perhaps in September, that Naren, on his way from Haridwar to Vrindavan, decided to take a train from Hathras. While on the platform, the stationmaster, Sharat Chandra Gupta, noticed him, asked if he was hungry and took him to his quarters to feed him. Thereafter, they embarked on a discussion of poetry and philosophy that both thoroughly enjoyed. Naren ended up staying in Hathras for several days during which Sharat invited his friends to meet him. On one of those days, Naren communicated his sadness about the plight of the Indian masses to Sharat who promptly asked if he could help in any way. Naren replied, 'Yes, take up the *kamandalu* (water jug) and go begging.' Sharat understood that Naren wanted him to give up his worldly interests and work for the good of many, and he did just that.

Later, Sharat would say, 'I followed those devilish eyes.' He gave up his career and the two left Hathras by train for Haridwar and from there proceeded to Rishikesh on foot. Here, Naren initiated Sharat into a life of renunciation and gave him the name Swami Sadananda. However, unused to the rigorous life of an ascetic, Sharat collapsed from exhaustion one day in a forest in Rishikesh. Naren carried his disciple on his back till he felt better. Both returned to Hathras from where Naren, after a bout of malaria, came back to Baranagore towards the end of 1888 and stayed there for almost a year. Sharat later joined Naren at Baranagore and remained attached to him till the end of his life.

At the end of 1889, Naren set out once more. He travelled to Vaidyanath and Allahabad, and during the third week of January 1890, to Ghazipur. It was here, while seeking a cure for pain due to lumbago, that he first came in contact with a saint called Pavahari Baba whom he grew to admire. From Ghazipur, he headed to Varanasi for the third time, probably in late March or early April of the same year. Here, he heard the sad news of Surendranath Mitra's serious illness and Balaram Bose's death. He was miserable and when his friend, Pramadadas Mitra, expressed surprise that a sannyasin like him should be so emotional, Naren retorted, 'Please do not talk that way. We are not dry monks. What! Do you think that because a man is a sannyasin, he has no heart?' Accordingly, he rushed back to Kolkata. Surendranath Mitra, the provider of the Baranagore Math, died on 25 May that year and Naren was greatly saddened by this loss.

In July 1890, Naren determined to set out once more and never return. He wanted to cut himself loose from the web of associations with the monastery, which were not very different from his family entanglements. However, before setting out on this round of travels, Naren wanted Sarada Devi to bless him. He found out that she was living in a village called Ghusuree across the river Ganga and paid her a visit. The meeting was overwhelming for both due to the memories of Sri Ramakrishna that each evoked in the other.

Naren told her, 'Mother, I shall not return until I have attained the highest *jnana*.'

'My son,' responded Sarada Devi, 'won't you see your own mother at home before leaving?'

'Mother, you alone are my mother!' was Naren's reply.

Although this was Naren's stance at this point, concern for his mother and her welfare would overwhelm him in later years.

Having now obtained Sarada Devi's blessings, he set out on his round of journeys once again. This time, however, he took along with him his brother-monk, Gangadhar, who was now known as Swami Akhandananda. The two men had always shared a deep bond, making Naren desirous of his company. The two went to Bhagalpur, Vaidyanath and Varanasi, and then to Ayodhya, Nainital and Almora.

It was at Almora, at the end of 1890 or the beginning of 1891, that Naren received the horrifying news that one of his younger sisters had committed suicide. Traumatized, he fled deep into the mountains to nurse his grief. There is speculation that this sister had burnt herself on her husband's funeral pyre, committing sati. Her identity, however, remains unclear; even Bhupendranath's biography does not mention her name. This incident, in all probability, fuelled Naren's outrage at the plight of

Indian women, expressed in several of his later lectures, and his desire to improve their condition, for which he was to take several concrete steps.

After Almora, Kedarnath and Badrinath in the Himalayas were next on the monks' agenda but Gangadhar fell ill at Rishikesh. Naren nursed him tenderly and eventually brought him to Tehri where the Diwan of Tehri-Garhwal, then a princely state, took care of them. From here, they went to Dehradun and, after Gangadhar had made a complete recovery, Naren sent him to Allahabad, meaning to go back to Rishikesh himself. It was here that Naren fell seriously ill and nearly died but was administered some local medicine by a tribal sadhu and managed to recover. When he was in good health again, he went to Meerut where many of his brother-monks had gathered and stayed there for five months.

At the end of January 1891, Naren set out alone for Delhi. He was there for three weeks and stayed for a part of the time with his friend, Dr H.K. Sen, and the rest at the house of an individual called Shyamaldas Seth in Roshanara Garden (which is now a school). While at Delhi, he held regular discussions with the Imam of the Fatehpuri Masjid who was an authority on the history of Chandni Chowk. Lala Hanwant Sahai, who was ten years old at the time and who later became a freedom fighter, recalled that the young monk 'was a man of frank views ... who could clinch an argument with a few words and a smile that seemed to enhance the spiritual glow on his face.' Apparently Naren, who preferred walking to any other mode of transport, would usually be followed everywhere by a group of boys who were impressed by his powerful build and fast pace.

Sometime in February 1891, Naren reached Alwar in Rajasthan where he stayed for seven weeks. Here, he formed a strong bond with a Muslim teacher of Urdu and Persian, and with many other Muslims of Alwar. They invited him to their homes with great affection and he shared many meals with them. An orthodox Hindu would have refused their hospitality but to Naren, whatever was offered with love and grace by anyone was welcome. Later, at Mount Abu, he stayed with a Muslim lawyer and refused his offer of making separate arrangements for his meals. Defending his stance, he later told a visitor, 'I am above all your social conventions . . .' I am not afraid of God because He sanctions it. I am not afraid of the scriptures because they allow it. But I am afraid of you people and your society. You know nothing of God and the scriptures . . . For me there is nothing high or low'. He would later remark that 'a junction of the two great systems, Hinduism and Islam' was the only hope for the country.

It was at Mount Abu, on 4 June 1891, that Naren first met Ajit Singh, the Raja of Khetri, with whom he was to form a lasting bond of friendship and mutual respect. In fact, it was the Raja who later conferred the name 'Vivekananda' on him by which he would be known in the West. This is the name by which he is known all over the world and in his own country today. After many involved conversations with Naren on spiritual themes, Ajit Singh was so impressed by him that he begged him to be his guest at Khetri. Naren agreed and spent over ten weeks at Khetri with his new friend. During this period, Ajit Singh began to regard Naren as his spiritual mentor. Naren, in turn, developed a deep affection for his host. This friendship was to be expressed in many crucial ways over the years.

After his visit to Khetri, Naren stayed for around two weeks at Ajmer again. When he left, many young people insisted on walking with him as far as he would let them as a token of farewell. Naren was deeply touched by this gesture. From Rajasthan, he now turned his attention to Gujarat. He visited several places here, prominently Porbandar, the birthplace of Mahatma Gandhi, where he stayed for eleven months.

Naren's next destination was Bombay (modern Mumbai) in Maharashtra. He arrived here at the end of 1892 and stayed for several weeks. He then travelled to Poona (modern Pune) where he stayed with the renowned leader, Bal Gangadhar Tilak, for eight to ten days. The two had met on the train from Mumbai to Pune and when Tilak had asked him his name, Naren simply said that he was a sannyasin. Impressed by the youthful monk, Tilak invited him home to stay.

Naren then went to Kolhapur and Belgaum, and finally turned his attention to the south. His desire was to visit Rameshwaram, which he called 'the Varanasi of southern India'. Accordingly, from Marmagaon (then a Portuguese colony), he came to Bangalore and, after staying there for a few days, travelled to Mysore, Trichur,

Cochin and Trivandrum some time in December 1892. When he was leaving Mysore, the ruler, Chamaraja Wodeyar, entreated him to accept some gifts. Naren protested but had to accept a beautifully carved pipe from him. Later, when he arrived in Madras (modern Chennai), Naren stayed with an old friend from Kolkata, Manmatha Nath Bhattacharya. He noticed Manmatha's cook looking admiringly at the pipe and promptly put it into his hands saying, 'Here, it is yours.'

Incidentally, there is another well-known instance of Naren's generosity that belongs to a much later period of his life. Once several young men, college students among them, had come to the Belur Math to converse with him. One of them admired the gold chain that Naren wore around his neck that was attached to a gold watch in his pocket and which had belonged to his father. Naren promptly put both the chain and watch in the amazed youth's hands and said, 'You like it! Then it is yours. But, my boy, do not sell it. Keep it with you as a souvenir.' The ease with which Naren parted with something so valuable and precious astounded everyone except those who knew this selfless man well.

To come back to his travels, before visiting Rameshwaram, Naren went to Madurai and from there to Kanyakumari, the very edge of India. It was here at the temple of the virgin goddess that Naren felt a powerful spiritual experience. Later, perched on 'the last bit of Indian rock', he conceived a plan to raise the Indian masses and give back to the nation its lost individuality. From here, at the beginning of 1893, he visited Ramnad, Rameshwaram, Pondicherry and then Madras. Later, 500 people came to the railway station in Hyderabad to receive him but when he left Hyderabad for Madras, a week later, over a thousand people came to see him off!

These years of travel left an indelible impression on Naren's mind. He had come to know the country intimately, and understood its strengths and problems like never before. The sharp division between India's glorious past and the present wretched reality struck him with great force. Most of his letters of that time talk of both aspects with passion and reflect his urge to rectify the evils that had beset Indian society. The conditions of abject poverty and ignorance under which the masses lived, and their exploitation by both the priests and the rich alike, as well as the degradation of women in Indian society, horrified him. Wherever he saw suffering, he responded to it personally, often with tears.

According to Naren, one of the biggest problems in Indian society was the practice of 'don't-touchism', another word to describe the impossibly rigid caste system that separated man from man and perpetuated atrocities on different groups of people. In his searing words, 'Monks and Sannyasins and Brahmins of a certain type have thrown the country into ruin. Intent all the while on theft and wickedness, these pose as preachers of religion! They will take gifts from the people and at the same time cry, "Don't touch me!" . . . If a potato happens to touch a brinjal, how long will the universe last before it is deluged? . . . For intricate problems like these they have been finding out scientific explanations for the last two thousand years—while one-fourth of the people are starving.'

According to Naren, the spiritual teachings of the Vedas and the Upanishads, and of the Buddha and other saints, had been twisted or ignored by priests who practised 'don't-touchism' rather than religion. What was needed, therefore, was to teach the masses the essence of Indian spiritual texts: that all life was one and was a manifestation of the divine. He noted, 'In religion lies the vitality of India, and so long as the Hindu race do not forget the great inheritance of their forefathers, there is no power on earth to destroy them . . . The more, therefore, the Hindus study the past, the more glorious will be their future . . .'

With equal fervour, Naren declared, '. . . all sorts of most demoniacal and brutal arguments . . . are brought forward in order to brutalise and tyrannise over the poor all the more . . . Our masses have been hypnotized for ages. To touch them is pollution, to sit with them is pollution! Hopeless they were born, hopeless must they remain. And the result is that they have been sinking, sinking, sinking, and have come to the last stage to which a human being can come . . . We are to blame. Stand up, be bold, and take the blame on your own shoulders '.

Naren believed that the root of all evils in India was the condition of the poor. He felt that the lower class needed to be given education in order to develop their lost individuality. As long as millions lived in hunger and ignorance, men who had been educated at their expense but who now ignored them were, in fact, traitors. Accordingly, he exhorted the people to consider the poor, the downtrodden and the ignorant as their God.

His denunciation of rituals was equally scathing. He condemned all those 'wretches' who spent ages pondering questions such as whether the bell should ring on the right or the left or how many times the light should be waved during prayers. In his opinion, all ceremonies should be done away with and 'the Living God, the Man–God', in short, every human being should be worshipped. The only way to do this was to spread ideas, to go from village to village and from door to door doing good to others.

In this, Naren was also criticizing the many reformers who talked of the need to discard harmful customs but did not show the slightest concern about the poverty and ignorance of the Indian masses. Although his thoughts cited above were actually expressed at a later date, Naren was already articulating them in his public lectures and letters written during his travels. Among some of his letters of this period that were written in Bengali, there is one asking a Vedic scholar of Varanasi to show him exactly where in the Vedas and Upanishads caste was sanctioned as hereditary.

Naren's travels through the country paralleled those of Mahatma Gandhi who undertook a similar journey through India to familiarize himself with all her aspects before undertaking to lead the Indian movement for independence from the British. Both, were powerful freedom fighters but while Gandhi fought in the political arena for freedom and sovereignty, Naren appealed to the Indians, particularly the youth, to regenerate themselves, free themselves from restraining shackles and achieve spiritual growth that would propel them towards progress.

Linked by travel

When Mahatma Gandhi returned to India from South Africa in January 1915, several people urged him to become active in Indian politics. However, Gandhiji had left India as a young man and had been away for two decades. In fact, he was probably more familiar with South Africa than India. Therefore, he decided to travel the length and breadth of his country to acquaint himself with all her aspects before he plunged into active politics.

Accordingly, Gandhiji began a long and painstaking journey across the land by train. He travelled by third-class compartments wherever he went so that he could interact with his fellow travellers in the crowded bogies. As news of his travels spread, people began to wait for him at railway stations, and he humbly accepted their words of welcome and offerings of flowers. Each step of his journey brought him closer to the reality of his country under British rule: poverty was rampant, particularly among the farmers, and a large majority of the people were illiterate.

The knowledge of his people and their circumstances that Gandhiji gained during this marathon tour was to form the basis of many of his later movements against the British. Thus, the desire to know their country intimately so that they could understand the people's problems and work for their welfare, no matter how uncomfortable the reality or difficult the journey, was a strong parallel between these two great men: Swami Vivekananda and Mahatma Gandhi.

7 🖼 The West and the East

It was at Porbandar that Naren first devised a concrete plan of going to the West to seek help for the revival of the Indian masses. The idea was probably suggested by Pandit Shankar Pandurang, a renowned Vedic scholar and the Diwan of the princely state of Porbandar. He was highly impressed by Naren's mastery of the Vedas and Upanishads, and of the Sanskrit language in general. During Naren's stay of eleven months with him, Pandit Pandurang told him, 'Swamiji, I am afraid you cannot do much in this country. Few will appreciate you here. You ought to go to the West where people will understand you and your worth.'

Preaching to the West, however, was not what Naren had in mind as he was mainly occupied with the regeneration of India. Nevertheless, he believed that his country could not survive if she cut herself off from the rest of the world. In a letter to one of his friends, he remarked, '. . . if India wants to raise herself once more, it is absolutely necessary that she brings out her treasures and throws them broadcast among the nations of the earth, and in return be ready to receive what others have to give her. Expansion is life, contraction is death. Love is life and hatred is death . . . We must mix, therefore, with all the races of the earth.'

The question of associating with the West had another dimension to it. From around 1813, when Christian missionaries began to arrive, India was attacked for being non-Christian, which, to many in the West, was synonymous with being uncivilized. By propagating Christianity in the country, the missionaries, therefore, believed that they were on a benevolent mission: they would rid Indians of their false religion and civilize them. From here, it was a short step to arguing that India had no political philosophy, no self-governing institutions, no idea of civic liberties and so on, thereby justifying British rule over the country.

Naren, who, in any case, could not tolerate the fact that India was under British domination, was also eager to prove to the world that these were lies as well as evidence of racial arrogance. In fact, he himself had experienced the conceit and condescending attitude of the British on several occasions. Once he was in the same train coach as two disdainful Englishmen. Both were engaged in criticizing everything that was Indian in the strongest possible language. Soon they began cracking jokes at Naren's expense. The young monk listened to them, outwardly unconcerned but seething within. When the train halted at a particular station, the Englishmen were shocked to hear Naren converse in perfect English with the stationmaster. Embarrassed, they asked him why he had not protested at their rude words about him seeing that he knew the language so well. Naren answered, in flawless English once again, 'It is not for the first time that I am seeing fools!'

It was at Kathiawar and later at Khandwa that Naren first heard of a Parliament of Religions to be held at Chicago in the United States of America in 1893. He decided to attend it. Although some of his admirers such as King Chamaraja Wodeyar of Mysore promptly offered to meet all his expenses in this regard, Naren politely declined their offers of help because he was not yet certain of his intention. However, after his visit to Kanyakumari and the shrine of the virgin goddess, where he had a vision of Sri Ramakrishna walking into the sea, beckoning him to follow and saying 'Go', he was certain about his future work and his destiny.

Accordingly, when he reached Madras, he was glowing with enthusiasm for his plan. Here, a group of young men gathered around him, of whom Alasinga Perumal, the headmaster of a high school attached to the Pachaiyappa's College, was the most prominent. He was to play a very significant role in Naren's future work and, in fact, many of the important letters that the monk wrote from America, outlining his experiences and future plans, were addressed to him. Once Naren's intention to attend the Parliament of Religions became known, there were many offers of financial help, some from the rich bankers of Madras. However, Naren was clear that the money for his trip had to come from the ordinary people on whose behalf he was going to the West. Accordingly, Alasinga Perumal went door to door with some others in order to raise the required money.

Meanwhile, Naren approached Colonel Henry Steel Olcott of the Theosophical Society to request a letter of introduction to the colonel's friends in America. Naren did so despite the fact that he disagreed with the Theosophists on several issues. Olcott refused to oblige him. In fact, the issue became rather messy because Olcott later denied that he had refused Naren the letter but some of his own colleagues who were present at the time contradicted him. They also tried to make amends for Olcott's churlish attitude by giving Naren introductions to their own friends in America. In any case, no one could deny that Naren always spoke the truth; his version of any event was bound to be the correct one.

While he was in the midst of these arrangements, Naren was visited by Munshi Jagmohanlal, private secretary to Raja Ajit Singh of Khetri. Ajit Singh's wife had given birth to a son, an event which they attributed to Naren's blessings. The couple wanted him to visit Khetri to bless the newborn and had sent Jagmohanlal to escort him. To the mystification and annoyance of those who were helping him with his trip to America, Naren promptly accepted this invitation and left Madras for Khetri with Jagmohanlal. They arrived there in the middle of April 1893, and Naren stayed with Ajit Singh and his family for three weeks.

This incident, apart from demonstrating Naren's selfless love for his followers, also highlighted an integral part of his personality: he was never in a hurry even when it seemed as if there was something urgent to do. This is an aspect that would surface time and again in America. The young monk, who preferred to walk everywhere, would often stop and talk as if time had stood still for him and those whom he addressed. On one occasion, when it was time for him to leave for a lecture because his audience was waiting eagerly, a little girl asked him how he wound his turban. Naren proceeded to give her a practical demonstration on the spot and no one dared hurry him until he had fully satisfied the child's curiosity.

While he was at Khetri, Naren's travel plans changed, for he was now to sail to America from Bombay and not Madras. A more memorable change was in his name: he was given the title 'Vivekananda' by Ajit Singh in May 1893 and he abandoned the names Swami Satchidananda/Vividishananda that he had occasionally used till then. Swami Vivekananda was now ready to face the world.

Vivekananda left Khetri on 10 May 1893 for Bombay with Jagmohanlal as his escort once more to see to his comfort and put him safely on the ship. En route, at the Abu Road railway station, he had an unexpected meeting with his brother-monks, Rakhal (Swami Brahmananda) and Hari (Swami Turiyananda). He briefly told them of his sorrow at the plight of the Indian masses and of his intention to alleviate them. It was an emotional encounter for all three of them, and Hari would later recall how their beloved Naren's voice was choked with feeling and cheeks wet with tears. He noted, 'Are not these the very words and feelings of

Buddha? . . . I could clearly perceive that the sufferings of humanity were pulsating in the heart of Swamiji—his heart was a huge cauldron in which the sufferings of mankind were being made into a healing balm.'

Vivekananda stayed in Bombay for over two weeks during which Jagmohanlal, on Ajit Singh's instructions, bought him a first-class ticket on the ship S.S. Peninsular and presented him with a new silk ochre robe and a handsome purse. Alasinga Perumal, too, had come from Madras to bid his leader a fond farewell and give him the money that he had been able to raise. Overwhelmed with gratitude at these gestures of love, Vivekananda boarded the ship on 31 May 1893. He carried with him his staff, his *kamandalu* and his coarse woollen blanket—his old, travel-weary companions. 'I have launched my boat in the waves, come what may,' he would later remark.

The young monk in his ochre robes was initially an object of curiosity for those aboard the ship and later one of reverence once facts regarding his awe-inspiring learning and scholarship became known. Vivekananda, in turn, delighted in the voyage, drinking in the new sights and sounds, and becoming acquainted with unfamiliar lands. In Colombo, for instance, he managed to visit the monasteries of the Hinayana Buddhists and, in Singapore, the haunts of the Malay pirates of yore. Hong Kong, Canton and Japan were the other ports that he visited.

His ship eventually docked in Vancouver, Canada, on 25th July. After spending the night here, he took a train to Winnipeg, then another to St Paul in the United

States and a third train to Chicago, his final destination, which he reached on 30 July 1893.

It was here that Vivekananda had his first frightening brush with reality that threatened to dislodge his ambitious spiritual plans. For some inexplicable reason, no one involved in his travel plans, including the young monk himself, had bothered to ascertain the practical details involved. Thus, Vivekananda learned that in order to be a delegate at the Parliament of Religions, he had to have some specific authority from those of the religious faith he represented. He carried no such credentials with him and even if he had, it was too late for him to be included in the list of delegates. Besides, he had arrived in Chicago six weeks before the Parliament was due to be held on 11 September. Again, no one had thought of finding out the exact date of this important event! It had also not occurred to anyone to find out the daily cost of living in a big American city. Chicago was an expensive city and the little money that Vivekananda had been provided with when he left India was disappearing fast. As he ruefully remarked to Alasinga in a letter, 'The expense I am bound to run into here is awful.'

Nevertheless, what at first appeared to be a disaster turned out to be a blessing in disguise. Each of these cases of oversight brought certain men and women into Vivekananda's life who would play a crucial role in his work and whose names would become inextricably linked with his story. Vivekananda refused to be defeated by the obstacles before him for he felt that he was executing a divine plan. Writing to Alasinga, he declared,

'All those rosy ideas we had before starting have melted, and I have now to fight against impossibilities. A hundred times I had a mind to go out of the country and go back to India. But I am determined, and I have a call from Above. I see no way, but His eyes see . . . I am here among the children of the Son of Mary, and the Lord Jesus will help me.'

Without wasting much time, Vivekananda took a train to Boston having learned that it was cheaper to live there. It so happened that an author, Katherine Sanborn, who had also taught at Smith College, was his companion on the train and they struck up a conversation. Impressed by him, she invited Vivekananda to be a guest at her farmhouse in Metcalf, Massachusetts, near Boston. He accepted willingly. She later described him as 'a magnificent specimen of manhood . . . with a lordly, imposing stride . . . and soft dark eyes that could flash fire if roused or dance with merriment if the conversation amused him.' She was also amazed by the fact that he spoke much better English than she did, was conversant with ancient and modern literature, and could recite pages of the Bible. To her, Vivekananda was 'an education, an illumination, a revelation.'

At her farmhouse, Breezy Meadows, Katherine introduced her guest to her friends and, in doing so, managed to fulfill a major part of his plan. One of the people she invited to meet Vivekananda was John Henry Wright, Professor of Greek Studies at Harvard University. The meeting could not occur at Katherine's place for some reason and so, Professor Wright invited the monk to spend the weekend with him at Annisquam, a seaside resort. A few conversations convinced Wright of his guest's worth and he immediately wrote to the director of the Parliament of Religions about Vivekananda not being included as a delegate because he lacked formal credentials. Arguing his case, Professor Wright remarked, 'He (Vivekananda) is more learned than all our learned professors put together.' Therefore, to insist on his producing credentials would be like asking the sun by whose right it shines.

These words of praise were enough to ensure that Vivekananda was included as a delegate to the Parliament of Religions, representing Hinduism. However, the young monk spoke to his first American public gathering not at Chicago but at the Boston Ramabai circle where he presented a picture of Hindu widows. He also spoke at a gathering at Annisquam village where his fierce denunciation of the British degradation of India was very well received. At the same time, he also spoke with frankness about the demeaning of India by the Indians themselves over centuries. Mary Tappan Wright, Professor Wright's wife, would later marvel at her guest's change from a passionate person in the grip of powerful feelings, as he appeared during his talks, to a happy childlike person while playing with her three children, Elizabeth, Austin and John.

Vivekananda's gratitude towards Professor Wright, whom he referred to as 'Adhyapakji' (teacher), for fulfilling his dream was expressed by him in several letters and messages. In one, he declared, 'You and your noble wife and sweet children have made an impression in my brain which is simply indelible and I thought myself so much near to heaven when living with you.' Meanwhile, leaving Annisquam on 28th August, he proceeded to Salem, Massachusetts, at the invitation of Kate Tannatt Woods, who had met him at Katherine Sanborn's house. An author and lecturer, she was also one of the founders of the Thought and Work Club of 1891, the first literary group of women in that town. Vivekananda stayed with her and her son, Prince, a medical student, from 29 August to 4 September.

Kate was a widow, and particularly fond of children. Once she invited a group of them to meet her guest and he regaled them with riveting stories of Indian animals, about children in Indian villages and the games they played. In Massachusetts, he also addressed the Thought and Work Club as well as scholars at the American Social Science Association at Saratoga Springs—and was equally comfortable with all three kinds of audiences. The young monk was to eventually form a lasting bond with his hosts. On his second visit to their place, he gave his monk's staff to Prince, and his woollen blanket and trunk to Kate, saying, 'Only my most precious possessions should I give to my friends who have made me at home in this great country.' These precious articles were preserved as souvenirs by the Woods family. Prince would later refuse to part with them to the British Museum which offered to buy them from him.

Meanwhile, when he was living with the Woods, Vivekananda was formally informed about his inclusion in the list of delegates at the Parliament of Religions and given an address at which he had to present himself the day before the event. Accordingly, he arrived in Chicago by train some time on 9th September. This is when another calamity of sorts occurred: Vivekananda discovered that he had lost the address of the office of the Parliament of Religions that he was to go to! Night was approaching and he could not make anyone at the railway station understand his problem, probably because he had approached the foreign immigrants there for help.

Lost and tired, he curled up inside an empty freight wagon in the railway yard and, with a prayer on his lips, went off to sleep. When he awoke the following morning, he started walking around in search of food to quell his hunger pangs. He covered a long distance from the railway yard and then began begging from door to door as he used to do in India. However, dark-skinned and unshaven as he was, and wearing crumpled ochre robes and a strange turban, he managed to rouse suspicions all around. He was turned away from every door and, in some cases, even insulted.

Undeterred but incredibly weary, Vivekananda continued to walk and eventually entered a street lined with beautiful homes. What happened next was nothing short of a miracle. Feeling that he could walk no longer, the monk sat down on the curb wondering what he was to do when, all of a sudden, a woman emerged from the house opposite and, coming up to him, asked, 'Sir, are you a delegate to the Parliament of Religions?' When he said that he was, she took him to her house, gave him some breakfast and then sent for his luggage from the railway station. Thereafter, she brought him to the office of the Parliament where the others awaited him.

Ellen George Hale, of 541 Dearborn Avenue was, therefore, closely linked with Vivekananda's story and the Hale family would remain the dearest to him among all the families that he would be associated with in the West. Thus it was that women seemed to play a crucial role in Vivekananda's plans in the West by welcoming him and coming to his aid when all other doors seemed closed. And some of their interventions did indeed seem part of a divine plan!

The Parliament of Religions

The Parliament of Religions was an adjunct or supplementary part of the World's Columbian Exposition, which had been organized in Chicago to celebrate the 400th anniversary of the discovery of America by Christopher Columbus. One of the main goals of the Exposition was to disseminate knowledge of progress in the world, especially in science and technology, that had been brought about by learned people in the West. Religion being an important aspect of human culture, it was decided to organize a Parliament of Religions along with the Exposition. The Reverend Dr John Henry Barrows, Professor of Comparative Religion in the

University of Chicago, was the originator and chairman of this Parliament.

The Parliament of Religions marked the first concerted effort to get the representatives of all religions of the world to share their views. Interestingly, however, the Archbishop of Canterbury, the senior bishop and principal leader of the Church of England, refused to send anyone to represent the Church of England at the Parliament of Religions because he could not even think of Christianity being on the same platform as other religions!

The centenary of this first Parliament of Religions was held once again in Chicago from 28 August to 4 September 1993. Over 6,500 delegates, representing around 125 religions, participated in it. Its major achievement was the formation of a group of the world's most influential religious leaders who were to demonstrate that religion can and should be a source of harmony rather than strife. This Parliament has led to a new series of conferences held in different parts of the world under the official title 'Parliament of the World's Religions'.

8 🖼 The Preacher and His Flock

A hush lay over the massive Columbus Hall. Seven thousand pairs of eyes from the hall below and the gallery above were trained on the long platform at one end where the distinguished representatives of various religions sat. There had been a grand procession at the beginning of the event when the curious men and women who had assembled there could see each member of the impressive line-up of speakers as they filed past. Many had spoken since then from prepared speeches and the audience had applauded them politely. There was, however, one who had not yet spoken and who seemed to have passed over several chances to do so. His attire and demeanour compelled their attention. In his silk ochre robes and turban, this magnetic presence exuded strength.

At long last, Dr Barrows, the master of ceremonies and the man behind this prestigious event, introduced Vivekananda who now rose to address the audience and his learned brethren. He had no paper in his hand and was clearly intending to speak extempore. The silence as he composed his thoughts was absolute; all breaths were hushed and faces turned eagerly towards him. And then, at last, he spoke. Surveying the gathering, he bowed his head and began with, 'Sisters and Brothers of America'. He could not proceed, thereafter, for the thunderous applause that followed his simple yet heartfelt greeting rang and echoed through the columns of the Hall, deafening all who were present. When Vivekananda resumed his speech after almost two minutes, he commanded everyone's attention as effortlessly as before. He was exhausted with emotion after his short address but it was obvious that the thirty-year-old monk had touched a chord in all hearts with his words on Hinduism and India's ancient spiritual heritage. The following day, all the dailies announced that his speech was the most popular one of the day and he thus became known to all of America in one stroke.

And so, the first part of Swami Vivekananda's plans came to pass. The Parliament of Religions that commenced on 11 September 1893 at Chicago was perhaps the first time that representatives of the major religions of the world were coming together to exchange views and expound their philosophies. Nearly seven thousand men and women had gathered in the famous Columbus Hall to hear the delegates speak and Vivekananda, who was formally representing Hinduism, had earlier suffered several nervous pangs at the thought of addressing such a huge and august gathering.

His first letter after the Parliament dated 2 October 1893, which was addressed to Professor Wright, his beloved adhyapakji, describes something of his trepidation at the time. He recalls: 'I was so, so afraid to stand before that great assembly of fine speakers and thinkers from all over the world and speak; but the Lord gave me strength, and I almost every day heroically faced the platform and the audience. If I have done well, He gave me the strength for it.' In another letter to Alasinga Perumal, he notes wryly that his heart 'was fluttering' and that his tongue 'nearly dried up'. For this reason, he declined to speak when his turn came several times over until he could postpone it no longer.

Even then, Vivekananda was remarkably humble and unassuming about the effect of his speech on the American people and the press. To Alasinga, he remarked, 'You would be astonished if I sent over to you the newspaper cuttings, but you already know that I am a hater of celebrity.' However, Vivekananda could not maintain a low profile any longer. He was now a public figure with droves of people clamouring to hear him and associate with his cause in some way. Never before had an 'Oriental' made such an impression on the people of America. He was, however, not the only person from Asia on the panel. Pratap Chandra Mazoomdar of the Brahmo Samaj, Annie Besant and G.N. Chakravarti of the Theosophical Society, and Anagarika Dharmapala of Ceylon (Sri Lanka) who represented Buddhism were also present.

Vivekananda's speech on the concluding day of the Parliament of Religions, 27 September 1893, indicating that all religions lead to the same God, took his audience by storm. He declared, 'If the Parliament of Religions has shown anything to the world, it is this: It has proved to the world that holiness, purity and charity are not the exclusive possessions of any church in the world . . . if anyone dreams of the exclusive survival of his own religion and the destruction of others, I pity him from the bottom of my heart . . .' He added that 'upon the banner of every religion will soon be written . . . "Help and not fight", "Assimilation and not Destruction", "Harmony and Peace and not Dissension".'

Later, in a talk that he gave at the People's Church, Washington D.C., on 28 October 1894, he said, 'Religion is not in books, not in forms, not in sects, not in nations: religion is in the human heart . . . It is love alone that can conquer hatred.' Meanwhile, after the Parliament, the most resounding vindication of Vivekananda's stance was provided by the newspaper *Herald*. It noted, 'Vivekananda is undoubtedly the greatest figure in the Parliament of Religions. After hearing him, we feel how foolish it is to send missionaries to this learned nation.'

Vivekananda, however, had not come to America to attain fame but to earn money for the regeneration of the poor and oppressed masses of India. His ambition was to set in motion a process by which help would be offered through men and women who would dedicate their lives to this end. In a letter to a friend, he noted, 'I am born to organize these young men . . . and I want to send them rolling like irresistible waves over India bringing comfort, morality, religion, education to the doors of the meanest and the most downtrodden. And this I will do or die.'

Accordingly, Vivekananda now began a series of lecture tours throughout America, having signed on with the Slayton Lyceum Bureau of Chicago. Soon he was travelling all over the mid-west and the east coast giving lectures on Indian philosophical heritage, and the meaning of religion and spirituality in the modern age. He also lectured with equal ease on Christianity and its varied aspects.

Among the places he visited were Iowa, Minneapolis, Detroit, Buffalo, Hartford, Boston, Cambridge, New York, Baltimore and Washington. The people who came to hear him ranged from policy-makers and the rich to the destitute and the lower rungs of society—and he made no distinction between them. In the winter of 1895, while in New York, Vivekananda rented rooms in a poor district of the city to hold classes. Some of his supporters protested because they felt that this would exclude the 'right kind of people' from his lectures. To this, he retorted, 'Where is the right kind and where is the bad? It is all *He*! In the tiger and the lamb, in the saint and the sinner, all *He*!'

The essence of Vivekananda's teachings was Vedanta, a system of philosophy based on the teachings of the Upanishads, the Bhagavadgita and the *Vedanta Sutra*, which he interpreted as a living philosophy: a feeling of oneness with all beings that was manifested through love for all. For this, it was essential to believe that every being was divine and that, therefore, to serve others was to serve God himself. Thus, to advance towards freedom—physical, mental and spiritual—and help others to do so was the 'supreme prize of man'. All faiths led to the same goal—a conviction that Sri Ramakrishna had experienced for himself. According to Vivekananda, there was only one basis 'of well-being, social, political, or spiritual—to know that I and my brother are *one*. This is true for all countries and all people.'

In his lectures in the West, Vivekananda was also encouraging people to rethink the values that had hitherto spread only fear and hatred among the followers of diverse religions. In this way, he not only paved the way for a dialogue between faiths but also with one's own self. Thus, although Vivekananda is often seen as the strongest challenge of Hinduism to Christianity and, by extension, to the British rule in India, he was also, in fact, the strongest Hindu challenge to what the Hindus had turned their religion into by questioning their oppressive social rules and rituals.

Meanwhile, the young monk was facing another physical challenge—that of the intense cold of America, another aspect he had neglected to consider before setting out on his journey to the West. To Alasinga, he wrote, 'Just now I have been to the tailor and ordered some winter clothing, and that would cost at least Rs 800 and up. And still it would not be good clothes, only decent . . .' He added, 'If I am to live longer here, my quaint dress will not do. People gather by hundreds in the streets to see me. So what I want is to dress myself in a long black coat, and keep a red robe and turban to wear when I lecture. This is what the ladies advise me to do . . .' He was also impatient with the criticism of orthodox Hindus that he was eating meat during his stay in America. He declared, 'If the people of India want me to keep strictly to my Hindu diet, please tell them to send me a cook and money enough to keep him ... As for me, mind you, I stand at nobody's dictation.'

Unfortunately, Vivekananda soon discovered that the lecture bureau had taken advantage of his simplicity and innocence and was cheating him. He was travelling long hours by train and giving innumerable lectures but they did not pay him even a fraction of what he had truly earned. Thomas Witherell Palmer of Detroit, one of his admirers, managed to release him from the bureau's clutches and, thereafter, Vivekananda conducted public lectures on his own. He also began holding classes for an ever-increasing number of people who were eager to seek spiritual truth. The American newspapers, meanwhile, regularly reported on his teachings and the enthusiastic response to them. Encouraged by the people's interest, Vivekananda established the Vedanta Society of New York as a non-sectarian organization to preach the universal principles of Vedanta with religious tolerance as its motto.

The young monk's success naturally earned him some enemies, prominent among whom were the Christian missionaries whose accounts of Hinduism and Indian civilization he had proved false. Furious at the consequent reduction in their funding, they sought to malign Vivekananda's character by portraying him as a fraud who was not recommended by anyone in India. Mazoomdar, now back in Kolkata and jealous of Vivekananda's success at the Parliament, joined this smear campaign and invented false stories about him.

Orthodox brahmanas whose tyranny he had exposed were quick to join in as well. The Theosophists, too, as well as Dharmapala of Ceylon targeted the young monk. The slander reached its peak in 1894 while Vivekananda was at Detroit.

However, at the same time, many liberal clergymen invited Vivekananda to speak in their churches and several of his new friends sprang to his defence. Mrs John Hudson Bagley, the wife of a former governor of Michigan, whose guest he was at Detroit, wrote two public letters declaring, 'He (Vivekananda) has given us in America higher ideas of life than we have ever had before ... He has been a revelation to Christians ... As a religious teacher and an example to all I do not know his equal ... He is a strong, noble being, one who walks with God ... He does not antagonize, but lifts people up to a higher level—they see something beyond man-made creeds and denominational names ...'

Vivekananda, whose travels and constant lectures were making him weary, and who also now began to feel the ravages of diabetes and asthma, was deeply pained by these false accusations. He did not mind the personal taunts as much as the anxiety he suffered on behalf of his American supporters whom he needed to assure that he was the voice of authentic Hinduism. He was also very worried about the effect these false stories would have on his aged mother back home. Accordingly, he requested Alasinga and his other followers to publicly endorse him and send reports of this to him so that he could silence his critics.

Consequently, a meeting to praise Vivekananda's efforts was held in Madras in April 1894 as well as in Bangalore in August, and the proceedings were sent to him. The report of the Madras meeting was published in some American newspapers, as also details of the extravagant praise accorded to him at a meeting held in Kolkata's Town Hall in September 1894. This reinforced Vivekananda's integrity and silenced his critics. He later warned his Indian followers to maintain a dignified silence before any detractors and not to resort to an unseemly 'tit for tat' attitude. 'I have been driven and worshipped by princes,' he wrote in a letter to a friend, 'I have been slandered by priests and laymen alike. But what of it? Bless them all. They are my very Self.'

Vivekananda's concern for women was another aspect that came to the fore during his travels though America. Marvelling at the difference between the status of women in India and America, he noted in a letter, 'It is the women who are the life and soul of this country (America) ... It is they who control social and civic duties. [here] Schools and colleges are full of women, and in our country women cannot be safely allowed to walk on the streets!' Struck by their independence and self-reliance, he declared, 'There is no chance for the welfare of the world unless the condition of women is improved. It is not possible for a bird to fly on only one wing.'

Hence, one of his plans for the future was to build a Math for women which would impart education to them and create conditions whereby they could work out their own destinies—much better, too, than men could ever do for them. This plan achieved fruition later. Meanwhile, his gratitude towards American women for befriending and supporting him, providing him with food, arranging for his lectures, and doing everything for his comfort and convenience was expressed in several of his letters. In one, he said, 'I shall never be able to repay in the least the deep debt of gratitude I owe to them.'

The young monk was to form enduring bonds of affection and friendship throughout this period. In fact, he had already formed a deep friendship with the family of the Lyons with whom he had been assigned to stay during the Parliament of Religions. Cornelia Conger, the granddaughter of John and Emily Lyon, recalled that the Lyons were worried that their guest might find American food bland and so, kept a bottle of tabasco sauce on the table at mealtimes, asking him if he would like a drop or two. Vivekananda promptly sprinkled a liberal amount on his food and, ignoring the Lyons' warning that the food would now be too hot, ate it with relish. Thereafter, a bottle of the sauce was always kept by his plate.

When he began to give lectures, people offered Vivekananda money for the work he hoped to do in India. Having no purse, he would bring it back tied in a handkerchief and pour it into Emily Lyon's lap to keep for him. Emily, fearful that her naïve guest might be cheated some day, taught him to differentiate between the coins, to stack them up neatly, to count them, and to keep a note of the amount each time. In a similar vein, Ellen Hale, who had rescued him from the street before the Parliament of Religions, opened a bank account to deposit the money that he was earning. She operated the account for him and sent him money whenever he needed it.

Another enduring bond formed by the young monk in America was with Sara Bull. A widow with an abiding interest in music and philosophy, she was to play a very important role in Vivekananda's life and work, and he came to consider her his spiritual mother. She gave liberally to the Vedanta societies that were later established in America and subsequently donated over one thousand rupees to the building of the Belur Math in India. Hearing Vivekananda speak in 1894, she immediately recognized his spiritual prowess and invited him to be her guest at Cambridge, Massachusetts. Here, he met Professor William Jones who had written extensively on religion and with whom he had many intellectual conversations.

Sara would later monitor all accounts of the money that Vivekananda and his disciples received for their work in America. From some of Vivekananda's letters to her, it is also revealed that she was sending money to help a cousin of his, who, however, remains unnamed. She would also eventually form a close bond with Swami Saradananda (Sharat) who came to America in 1896 to help his mentor in his work. Sara undertook to finance the education of Saradananda's two brothers as well. Her most remarkable gesture, though, was to send to the monastic disciples of Sri Ramakrishna who had served the saint's mother, Chandradevi, till her death, a donation to provide a home within the Belur Math for their mothers.

Another admirer of Vivekananda was Dr Egbert Guernsey, an eminent physician, writer and editor based in New York. He wrote to Sara Bull that the young monk ' … by the kindness of his heart, great intelligence, purity and nobility of character has endeared himself to me almost like a son …' A Frenchwoman, Marie Louise, and Leon Landsberg, a journalist, were two other admirers. In fact, Vivekananda even initiated them into sannyasa, conferring the names of Swami Abhayananda and Swami Kripananda on them, respectively, to the puzzlement of many of his followers. Both, however, turned against him in course of time and became his critics. Landsberg, for instance, felt that his mentor ought not to devote so much attention to cooking food and other 'unworthy' pursuits. Vivekananda, however, continued to talk of them with love and affection.

Sarah Ellen Waldo, a lover of philosophy, who recorded Vivekananda's lectures in New York in longhand, was another close associate. He would later exclaim to her, 'How could you have caught my thoughts and words so perfectly? It was as if I heard myself speaking!'

Two sisters, Josephine MacLeod and Betty Sturges, heard the young monk's lecture in New York and were instant converts to his philosophy, especially the former. Josephine later recalled, 'It is the Truth that I saw in Swamiji that has set me free … It was like the sun that you will never forget once you have seen.' She believed him to be 'the new Buddha'. Josephine was one of the few to whom Vivekananda would write about his innermost thoughts, which he concealed even from his closest brother-monks. Josephine and Sara Bull later became great friends, united as they were in their love for 'our Prophet' and their desire to spread his message of Vedanta.

Betty's future husband, Francis Leggett, a rich businessman, was another wholehearted admirer of the young monk. There is an interesting story about Vivekananda's stay with this couple at their home, Ridgely Manor, in the Hudson river valley north of New York City. After meals, the young monk would often go for a walk but if he heard that ice-cream was to be served, he would instantly sit down again with a huge smile of anticipation on his face. Thereafter, he would devour large quantities of it. He also enjoyed cooking for his friends and would often return from a lecture and rush into the kitchen with childlike enthusiasm to prepare their meal.

Josephine, however, was often impatient with Vivekananda for not charging any fee for his classes unlike his public lectures. Once when there was not enough money to pay the rent for his lodgings in New York, she announced to the class, 'Everyone is going to pay ten cents.' Her friend promptly stopped her, saying, 'Religion is not for sale.' And yet somehow, perhaps by a divine design, whenever it seemed as if money was at an end, some benefactor or the other would turn up eager to hear Vivekananda's words and would be more than willing to contribute to his upkeep, financially or otherwise.

In the summer of 1895, Vivekananda went to Thousand Island Park to a retreat that Mary Elizabeth Dutcher, an artist, had organized for a select few. This was a welcome respite from his hectic schedule and the young monk enjoyed himself here immensely. Here too, he had to deal with a stream of admirers, prominent among whom were Christine Greenstidel and Mary C. Funke, both of whom had heard him at Detroit and had travelled seven hundred miles in the night and in the rain to be with him. They told him, 'We have come, just as we would go to Jesus if he were still on earth and ask him to teach us.' Moved, Vivekananda replied, 'If only I possessed the power of the Christ to set you free now.'

Mary Funke's reminiscences reveal the 'fun-loving' side of this 'powerful saint'. He would cook for everyone using various spices and grin with amusement when they struggled to eat the delicious but exceedingly 'hot' food. Sometimes he would stand with a white napkin draped over his arm like the waiters in dining cars and, mimicking them perfectly, would shout, 'Last call fo' the dining cah. Dinner served.' And then, during dinner, he would gently poke fun at the eccentricities of one or the other, which he had already discovered with his all-too-perceptive eye.

Among the various anecdotes regarding Vivekananda's stay in America, there is one that stands out for showing the amazing abilities of concentration and focus that he possessed. On one occasion, he was walking past a river when he saw a group of boys trying to shoot some balloons in the water but failing to hit their target every time. Vivekananda asked them why they were unsuccessful in their task and the boys told him that aiming and shooting at a moving object was near-impossible. Irritated by his smile, they placed a revolver in his hand and challenged him to shoot the balloons. Vivekananda aimed at and shot each balloon in turn with perfect ease. He then explained to the awestruck boys that he had focused all his concentration on the balloons and 'could not see or think of any other thing'. The same attention and single-minded focus marked every task that Vivekananda undertook throughout his life.

About Sara Bull

Sara Bull, along with a later disciple of Vivekananda, Sister Nivedita, was associated with the Indian scientist, Jagadis Chandra Bose, who is now regarded as India's first modern scientist. Known as the pioneer of experimental science in India and a brilliant inventor, he devised many instruments for his research in physics and physiology. However, at an early stage in his career, the struggling Bose was supported by Sara against efforts to suppress his work by the British. Both Sara and Sister Nivedita nursed him during his subsequent illness in 1900. Later, Sara gave Bose $4,000 to set up his botanical research laboratory and was thereby instrumental in fulfilling his dreams of becoming a renowned scientist. Unfortunately, Bose did not ever publicly acknowledge Sara's crucial help even during the opening of the Bose Research Institute in Kolkata in 1917, which, ironically, had been largely financed by Sara.

Similarly, Bose never spoke of the considerable debt he owed Sister Nivedita, who actively encouraged him to pursue scientific research and helped him financially. Her support to Bose was, however, acknowledged by the poet laureate, Rabindranath Tagore, who noted that 'in the day of his success, Jagadis gained an invaluable energizer and helper in Sister Nivedita and in any record of his life's work, her name must be given a place of honour.'

9 🕉 Taking the World and Home by Storm

On 14 August 1895, Vivekananda sailed from New York to Europe. After attending the wedding of Berry Sturges and Francis Leggett in Paris, he arrived in London and stayed there from 10 September to 27 November 1895. This was an emotionally-charged period for him. On the one hand, he was in the land of the British rulers of India whose domination over his people he resented. However, on the other, this was also the land of John Stuart Mill and Herbert Spencer, the philosophers whose thoughts had inspired him since adolescence.

The people of England, too, were curious about this young monk whose fame had spread so quickly. Accordingly, there was a considerable audience for his talk at the Prince's Hall in London on 22 October. Afterwards, it was apparent to everyone that Vivekananda was not a sectarian monk or a missionary of Hinduism. He had touched their minds and hearts with truths that were truly universal. The *Westminster Gazette* that published an interview with him on 23 October described his face as one that lit up 'like that of a child, it is so simple, straightforward and honest.' In response to a question, Vivekananda clarified that his teaching was his own interpretation of ancient books in the light that his mentor, Sri Ramakrishna, had shed on them.

Although his first stay in England was short, Vivekananda was to make one more journey to this country later from 20 April to 16 December 1896. Both visits forced him to revise his views of the British. Once he had regarded them with hatred and disdain, but after a close association with several aspects of English national life, he now discovered their industry and mettle, their ability to be 'bold, brave and steady', their 'immense practicality', and 'immense vitality'. In a letter to Mary Hale, daughter of Ellen Hale, he confessed, 'My ideas about the English have been revolutionalised . . . They are steady, sincere to the backbone, with great depths of feeling.'

The young monk made one of his most important associations in England in the person of Margaret Noble, an Irishwoman, who was to follow him to India and become his spiritual daughter, under the name of Sister Nivedita. She was to make a stellar contribution to the education and progress of the women of India, a task that Vivekananda specifically entrusted her with. Margaret had a passion for justice, freedom and truth. She found these echoed in her mentor's words whom she met for the first time on 10 November 1895 at the house of her friend, Lady Isabel Margesson.

Incidentally, Lady Henrietta Ripon, wife of Lord George Ripon, who had been the viceroy of India from 1880–1884, was one of those whom Lady Isabel had invited to hear Vivekananda speak. Margaret was immensely moved by the young monk's words and felt as if her quest for the truth had ended. Before Vivekananda left London for America, he revealed his plans for the education of Indian women to her with his usual intensity and she found herself saying, 'I will help you.' 'I know it,' was his instant reply.

At this point, Vivekananda was confronted, all of a sudden, with family concerns once more. His younger brother, Mahendranath (also called Mohin), who was now twenty-six years old, arrived in London in the summer of 1896, wanting to study law and become a lawyer. Mohin stayed with his brother at Pimlico in London where the latter was living and holding his classes. There were others with him in the same establishment: E.T. Sturdy, who had practised asceticism and knew about the Vedas; Henrietta Muller, who had met Vivekananda in America; Josiah John Goodwin, a professional stenographer who had accompanied the monk from America, dedicated his life to him and recorded all his lectures between December 1895 and December 1896; and Swami Saradananda (Sharat) who had come to the West some time ago to assist in his mentor's work.

Vivekananda was troubled by his brother's decision and even sought Sara Bull's advice on the matter. He did not want Mohin to become a lawyer but to study the science of electricity instead and to go to America for this purpose. However, Mohin was stubborn and, having discovered the joys of the Reading Room at the British Museum, spent most of his time there studying books on law. Another kind of trouble was brewing, meanwhile, in the household at Pimlico. Sturdy began to feel that Vivekananda showed no signs of asceticism and was merely enjoying the luxuries provided by his Western friends. Henrietta, on the other hand, was a strongly opinionated person, and made no bones about her dislike for both Sturdy and Mohin. In fact, she would later turn against Vivekananda, too, for his continued ill-health, as, according to her, no spiritual person ought to be ill. Meanwhile, Vivekananda was compelled to send Mohin away from the household to prevent any clashes between the inmates.

His distress over these happenings was, however, lessened to some extent by the Reverend Hugh Reginald Haweis, Curate of the St James's Church at Marylebone in London. He had given two sermons in his church on the importance of Vivekananda's teachings. He also sent Vivekananda a collection of his own sermons, inscribing the book thus: 'To the Master Vivekananda from one who both reverences and admires his teachings.' Proof indeed that greatness and its acknowledgement was not confined to country, status or profession!

Another cheering episode for the young monk was his meeting on 28 May at Oxford with Professor Max Mueller, the renowned German Indologist, who had translated the Rig Veda and other important texts. Vivekananda was delighted to learn that Professor Mueller was collecting the sayings of Sri Ramakrishna and writing a book on his life. For Max Mueller, it was an honour to meet the famed saint's closest disciple.

Another very close bond formed by Vivekananda in England was with Charlotte Elizabeth Sevier and her husband, Captain James Henry Sevier, a non-commissioned officer of the British army. This occurred during his second visit. After listening to one of his lectures, Captain Sevier asked Josephine MacLeod, 'Do you know this young man? Is he really what he seems?' Josephine answered 'yes' to both queries and Captain Sevier then said, 'In that case, one must follow him and with him find God.' The couple would eventually follow Vivekananda to India and help establish the Advaita Ashram at Mayavati, Almora, thereby giving shape to the young monk's 'Himalayan dream' of founding a monastery in these mountains where his Indian and Western disciples could live together.

Meanwhile, concerned at Vivekananda's failing health, brought about by his strenuous exertions to raise money for his work in India, the Seviers took him to Switzerland on 31 July 1896 so that he could recover. Henrietta Muller accompanied them but eventually returned to London towards the end of August. Delighted at the prospect of seeing snow and wandering along mountainous paths, Vivekananda's health revived, and he felt as full of energy and enthusiasm as before. Always fond of walking, he found numerous opportunities to indulge this passion in the Alps. Geneva, Montreux, Lucerne, Zermatt and Schaffhausen were among the places he visited. In fact, it was in a village at the foot of the Alps between Mont Blanc and St Bernard that he conceived the idea of establishing a monastery in the Himalayas.

On his return, Vivekananda initially stayed with Henrietta at her house in Wimbledon and then shifted to 39, Victoria Street in London. Greatly refreshed after his holiday, he began to hold classes there with renewed vigour. Meanwhile, Kali (Swami Abhedananda) had come to England in response to Vivekananda's summons and was now with him, helping him in his work. Vivekananda's letters to Alasinga, his brother-monks and his American friends at this stage reflect his vision and consequent desire for a society without differences where man would be free in all matters. They also reflect his yearning for his beloved country, India, the land that he sorely missed and craved to return to. In one, he remarked, 'I am a dreamer, a visionary; but believe at least that I am sincere to the backbone . . . I love my country only too, too well.' He later declared, 'India I loved before I came away. Now the very dust of India is holy to me, the very air is now to me holy.'

Accordingly, on 16 December 1896, Vivekananda, accompanied by the Seviers, Henrietta and Goodwin, set sail for India on the Prinz Regent Luitpold, which was heading from Naples to Ceylon. He reached Colombo on 15 January 1897 where he stayed for four days, and was given a rousing reception by both Buddhists and Hindus alike. Thereafter, he crossed the sea to reach the mainland of India and visited, in turn, Rameshwaram, Ramnad, Madurai and Kumbakonam. At each of these places, he was publicly honoured for his work in the West. At Ramnad, for instance, the Raja of Ramnad, his follower, helped to unhitch the horses from Vivekananda's carriage and then drew the carriage along with some others. The young monk was almost moved to tears by this gesture.

At Madras, where Vivekananda stayed from the 6 to 15 February, the reception was the most enthusiastic. Many of his admirers and disciples from Bengal and north India had come here to await his arrival. Hundreds of people had gathered at a small railway station near Madras to see him. The crowd forced his train to an unscheduled stop by flinging themselves on to the track. Thousands of people flooded the railway station as his train steamed in. He was greeted with applause and cheers and whisked away into a triumphal procession through the streets of Madras that had been profusely decorated for the purpose. Vivekananda was later honoured in a public meeting and gave several lectures to the people during his nine-day stay in the city. Deeply touched and even astonished at the people's adulation and his obvious popularity, he was, however, far too great a man to be unduly swayed by this.

The newspapers, too, carried several articles in praise of the young monk and his work. For instance, the editorial in the *Indian Mirror* of 21 January 1897 noted, 'We cannot yet understand the far-reaching consequences of the work which Vivekananda has achieved . . . but we may take it upon ourselves to say that Vivekananda has forged the chain, which is to bind the East and the West together—the golden chain of a common sympathy, of a common humanity, and a common and universal religion.' Thus, Vedanta, as preached by the young monk, would forge a relationship of love and understanding between the East and the West. The editorial ended thus: 'Can humanity, then, ever be too thankful to Vivekananda? Can his fellow-countrymen be ever too proud of him or be ever too grateful to him?'

And yet, there were words of criticism being levelled at Vivekananda as well, perhaps fuelled by the frenzied welcome he had received. In his Madras address, he had mentioned that the Indian Theosophists had joined the American Christian missionaries in spreading lies about him. This was a mere statement of fact, the plain truth—but some of the Theosophists renewed their campaign of slander against him, as did P.C. Mazoomdar, the Brahmo leader in Kolkata, once more. Vivekananda had already instructed Rakhal (Swami Brahmananda) in a letter, 'Take no notice of Mazoomdar's madness. He surely has gone crazy with jealousy.' Trying to make light of his enemies to comfort his agitated followers, he later remarked that as he had received a great deal of love from the world, he deserved some amount of hatred as well.

Physically exhausted and longing for his hometown, Vivekananda left Madras by boat for Kolkata and arrived there on 19 February 1897. A special train brought him from the Budge Budge landing to the Sealdah railway station the next morning where he was given a tumultuous welcome by an enthusiastic crowd. Triumphal arches had been erected and there was a huge procession to honour him. On 28 February, a public reception was held with over five thousand people clamouring to see Vivekananda.

It was on 1 May 1897 that Vivekananda established the Ramakrishna Mission Association, thus providing an enduring order for his brother-monks and disciples. Justifying its existence, he declared, 'From my travels in various countries, I have come to the conclusion that without organization nothing great and permanent can be done.' This new order was to fulfill his dream of sending men and women to the poor and oppressed masses of the country to alleviate their condition. This was a turning point in the lives of the monks. Hitherto, their ideal was to strive for personal freedom or *mukti* and the realization of God by penance and meditation, remaining aloof from the world and its concerns. Now, however, Vivekananda was insisting that they serve the poor, the helpless and diseased, seeing God in them, and inspire others to do the same. This was the mission of his life—to create a new order of sannyasins in India who would dedicate their lives to help and save others.

Predictably, some of the monks were not comfortable with the introduction of Western ideas of social action, public good and organization into Sri Ramakrishna's teachings. However, a reproach by Swami Yogananda to this effect provoked one of Vivekananda's most well-known outbursts. 'What do you understand of religion?' He thundered at the monks, 'You are only good at praying with folded hands: "O Lord! How beautiful is Your nose, how sweet are Your eyes," and all such nonsense; and you think that your salvation is secured ... As if God-realisation is such an easy thing to be achieved! ...You think you understand Shri Ramakrishna better than myself! ...You want to preach Ramakrishna as you have understood him which is mighty little! Hands off !'

So saying, he fled to his room only to return a while later, his anger gone. Addressing the overwrought monks, he said, '... I cannot think or talk of Shri Ramakrishna long without being overwhelmed ... I am a slave of Ramakrishna, who left his work to be done by me and will not give me rest till I have finished it! And, oh, how shall I speak of him! Oh, his love for me!' Thereafter, there were no more protests from the monks: they might not have understood him entirely but they loved Vivekananda as he loved them, and they believed, now more than ever before, that Sri Ramakrishna was working through his beloved Naren.

Max Mueller and India

Professor Friedrich Max Mueller (1823–1900) was one of the founders of the western academic field of 'Indian studies' and the discipline of comparative religion. Mueller wrote both scholarly and popular works on the subject of Indology (in other words, Indian history, literature and culture), making Indian philosophical thought available to the West. In fact, his first book was a German translation of the *Hitopadesa*, a collection of Indian fables.

At the time, the Vedic language Sanskrit, was thought to be the oldest of the Indo-European languages. Mueller, therefore, devoted himself to the study of this language, becoming one of the major Sanskrit scholars of his day. He believed that the earliest documents of Vedic culture should be studied in order to understand the development of religious belief in general. He even moved to England in 1846 in order to study Sanskrit texts in the collection of the British East India Company.

While there, Mueller persuaded the Company to allow him to undertake a critical edition of the Rig-Veda, a task he pursued doggedly over many years (1849–1874). He is most remembered for this work. The *Sacred Books of the East,* a massive, fifty-volume set of English translations of Asian religious writings, was later prepared under his direction.

Mueller was greatly impressed by Ramakrishna Paramahansa, and authored several essays and books on him. He also had links with the Brahmo Samaj in India.

Mueller eventually became the leading commentator on the culture of India, which Britain then controlled as part of its empire. His papers and correspondences have been preserved at the Bodleian Library in Oxford. The Goethe Institutes in India that promote the German language and encourage cultural exchange are each named the Max Mueller Bhavan in his honour.

10   More Travels and Travails

Vivekananda's exertions in the West had taken a severe toll on his health. His asthma bouts were becoming more and more frequent, especially in Kolkata's humid climate. At the time, the monks were staying at the Alambazar Math where he continued to give lectures on Vedanta to the hundreds of people who thronged there every day. However, he now decided to travel within his country once more. Accordingly, from May 1897 till the end of that year, he travelled and lectured extensively in places like Lucknow, Punjab, Kashmir, Jammu, Dehradun, Bareilly and Ambala. Wherever he went, apart from his words on Vedanta and India's glorious spiritual heritage, he also advised people, particularly the youth, to rebuild their individual characters. The strength of the nation, he said, depended upon the strength of the individual. He wanted men with 'nerves of steel and muscles of iron', with 'force of character', 'not cowards but lions', who would dedicate their lives to India's masses.

Vivekananda also visited Almora on the advice of his physicians who felt that its cool, dry air would revive his health. Writing from here to a friend, he said, 'I have begun to take a lot of exercise on horseback, both morning and evening. Since then I have felt very much better indeed . . .' However, he soon began to get restless at his enforced idleness. In a letter to Gangadhar (Swami Akhandananda), he declared, 'Work, work, work—I care for nothing else. Work, work, work, even unto death! . . . I am a fighter and shall die in the battlefield.' Perhaps he had an inkling that he would die sooner than expected, for in another letter to Gangadhar, he said, 'The body must go, no mistake about that. Why then let it go in idleness? . . . Don't be anxious even when I die, my very bones will work miracles . . .'

He returned to Kolkata in January 1898. The Math now shifted to a garden-house belonging to an individual called Nilambar Mukherjee on the western bank of the Ganga at Belur. Land was also purchased at Belur where Vivekananda wanted to build a permanent Math. Raja Ajit Singh of Khetri had already made a handsome donation towards this end; so had Henrietta Muller who donated the entire amount for purchasing the land. With support pouring in, work progressed quickly and eventually, the Belur Math was consecrated on 9 December 1898 and became the permanent headquarters of the Ramakrishna Order.

Meanwhile, the order was to receive one of its greatest members from overseas who would do all in her power to improve the conditions of women's education. In a letter to Margaret Noble dated 29 July 1897, Vivekananda said, 'Let me tell you frankly that I am now convinced that you have a great future in the work for India. What was wanted was not a man, but a woman;

a real lioness, to work for the Indians, women specially.' After warning her about the difficulties she would face in India in terms of the 'fearfully hot' climate, and the superstitions and suspicions of the people, he added, 'If in spite of all this, you dare venture into the work, you are welcome, a hundred times welcome.'

Margaret responded to his plea with alacrity and arrived in Kolkata on 28 January 1898. Vivekananda was at the docks to receive this courageous woman who had given up everything to pursue his vision. On 25 March, he initiated her into the Ramakrishna Order and gave her the name 'Nivedita' or 'the dedicated'. When the ceremony ended, he asked her to pay homage to the Buddha who, in his view, was worthy of emulation because in his varied incarnations he had sacrificed his life several hundred times for others. She established the Nivedita Girls' School in Kolkata that was formally inaugurated on 13 November 1898, the beginning of her work in India.

Nivedita was, however, to experience many initial clashes with her mentor, particularly over his attempts to Indianize her. He asked her to forget her country, her past, her family and even her original name so that she could assimilate herself better with the Indian people whom she was meant to serve. This was a difficult proposition for the strong-willed Nivedita, yet she tried hard to do so for her mentor's sake. In a letter to a friend, she remarked, 'I cannot yet throw any of my past experience of human life and human relationships overboard. Yet I can see that the saints fight hard to do so—can they be altogether wrong?' That Nivedita held her mentor in awe is clearly illustrated by several episodes, a prominent one being their visit to the cave of Amarnath in Kashmir in August 1898 when she saw him experience 'a great exaltation' before the sacred ice Shiva-linga. She did not always understand him but would later say, '. . . the fact is that anyone can see that I worship him—and that's the truth.'

That Vivekananda considered women as the redeemers of civilization is made amply clear in his plea to Nivedita to adopt his country's women and also through many of the latter's writings. For instance, in one of her letters to Josephine MacLeod, she observes, 'What ideals of womanhood Swami holds! . . . As I read over the things he has said to me of them, I realize that it is all, every word of it, a trust for the women of the whole world's future—but first and chiefly for them of his own land . . .'

Earlier, during his stay in America, Vivekananda had written to Tarak (Swami Shivananda) about his desire to secure a place for Sarada Devi, Sri Ramakrishna's widow. They all referred to her as 'Mother', and regarded her as a personification of the goddess. However, it was not until 2 December 1954 that the Sri Sarada Math of Vivekananda's dream would come into being.

In March 1898, when Vivekananda was at Darjeeling for a brief respite, he received news about the outbreak of plague in Kolkata. He returned immediately and plunged himself into relief work along with his brother-monks who shared his belief that true spirituality lay in working for others. A plot of land was rented to house a relief camp and Vivekananda personally oversaw its functioning. It was only when the plague threat had completely disappeared that he and his monks relaxed their labours. Needless to say, his health deteriorated even further as a result of these exertions on behalf of the people. Additionally, soon after, the news of the deaths of Pavahari Baba whom he revered and J.J. Goodwin whom he loved dearly were staggering blows and he grieved their loss deeply.

For some time now, Vivekananda's friends in the West had been urging him to pay them another visit. Disregarding health concerns, he determined to undertake the journey for a second time to earn more money in the service of India and to teach whoever was seeking spiritual truth. Accordingly, on 20 June 1899, Vivekananda, accompanied by Nivedita and Hari (Swami Turiyananda), set sail from Kolkata on the S.S. Golconda. Their visit had been sponsored by Josephine MacLeod. During this trip, Nivedita intended to create interest in the education of Indian women among their Western counterparts and also to raise funds for the school for girls that she had established in Kolkata.

Their ship entered Tilbury Dock on the Thames River in London on 30 July 1899. Christine Greenstidel and Mary Funke, his earlier companions at Thousand Island Park, had crossed the Atlantic to receive Vivekananda. He stayed in Wimbledon for a fortnight, a part of which was spent with Nivedita's family—her mother, sister, May, and brother, Richmond—all of whom welcomed him with open arms. On 17 August, Hari, Christine and Mary accompanied Vivekananda by boat from Glasgow to New York.

During this second visit, Vivekananda lectured mostly in northern and southern California, staying at San Francisco, Alameda, Pasadena and Los Angeles, in turn. His message of Vedanta and of regeneration was greeted with as much enthusiasm as before and crowds flocked to hear him speak. The newspapers were full of praise once again for this tireless monk and his teachings. Vivekananda's lectures were as inspiring and passionate as always. However tired or ill he was feeling, his face seemed to radiate a divine light when he spoke—and this was noticed by all.

New York, Detroit and Chicago—three cities for which he nurtured a special fondness—were also on his itinerary. Tragedy had struck the Hale family some months prior to his visit: George Hale had died and the remaining family no longer lived at Dearborn Avenue but was scattered. In June 1900, Vivekananda made what he knew would be his last visit to Mary Hale, George's daughter, with whom he corresponded regularly. He had earlier told her after her father's death, '. . . if it were possible to exchange grief, and had I a cheerful mind, I would exchange mine for your grief ever and always.' This particular visit was fraught with emotion and when they parted, he remarked, 'Oh, it is so difficult to break human bonds!'

Vivekananda's hectic schedule during this visit was beginning to ravage his body and he could not ignore this any longer. He had now started suffering from neurasthenia, a disease of the nerves. Moreover, his asthma was so acute that he often gasped for breath. Thus, many of his letters during this period reflect his desire to rest awhile and focus on his health. He had once noted, 'I was born for the life of a scholar—retired, quiet, poring over my books. But the Mother dispenses otherwise.' He now wrote to Rakhal (Swami Brahmananda), 'Kindly pray to the Mother that I do not have to shoulder all this trouble and burden any longer. Now I desire a little peace . . .'

In addition, he was also deeply saddened when Kali (Swami Abhedananda), who had been brought over from London to take care of the Vedanta teaching in New York, disrupted the smooth functioning of the Vedanta Society of New York by insisting on being its spiritual and organizational head. He had also been unpleasant towards Sara Bull to whom Vivekananda had entrusted all the organizational Vedanta work in America. In fact, disgusted with Abhedananda, Francis Leggett resigned from the presidentship of the society that he had done so much to nurture. Vivekananda, however, deliberately decided not to intervene in this matter 'for fear of making further trouble'.

It was in the light of all these concerns that Vivekananda decided to renounce his place in the order that had now started working smoothly. By a legally registered will, he transferred his power over the property and organization of the Ramakrishna Math and Mission to Rakhal and others in succession. The trust deeds were executed on 25 August 1900 at the British Consulate in Paris and were sent to Kolkata.

Thereafter, Vivekananda wrote to Nivedita, 'Now I am free, as I have kept no power or authority or position for me in the work . . . The Math etc. belong now to the immediate disciples of Ramakrishna except myself. I am so happy a whole load is off me . . . I have served Ramakrishna through mistakes and success for twenty years now. I retire for good and devote the rest of my life to myself . . .'

Vivekananda now journeyed to Paris to attend a Congress of the History of Religions organized by the Sorbonne University to which he had been invited. Incidentally, Professor Max Mueller was also among the invitees but could not be present owing to his ill-health. Vivekananda gave a talk at the Congress on 7 September 1900 which was received with much acclaim. Thereafter, Josephine MacLeod introduced her friend to various royal personages who had come to Paris for the Great Exposition that was being held at the same time. To Vivekananda, however, the poor and unknown of Paris were probably of much greater interest.

While in Paris, Vivekananda wrote a letter, mostly in French, to Christine Greenstidel, saying, 'I have had many difficulties, and also some very great successes. But all my difficulties and suffering count for nothing, as I have succeeded. I have attained my aim. I have found the pearl for which I dived into the ocean of life. I have been rewarded. I am pleased. Thus it seems to me that a new chapter of my life is opening.'

Vivekananda remained in Paris for three months and then accepted an invitation from Emma Calve, a renowned French singer who admired him, to tour Egypt with her. Apart from them, the party comprised several people among whom were Josephine MacLeod and Hiram Maxim, the inventor of the machine gun. Nivedita had stayed behind with Sara Bull in Brittany. The group left Paris on 24 October 1900 by the Orient Express, stayed over in Vienna for three days, and then travelled through eastern Europe to Constantinople (modern Istanbul) and then to Cairo. Vivekananda thoroughly enjoyed the journey and wrote detailed impressions of it in Bengali.

However, halfway into the journey, he was hit by a sudden desire to return to his homeland and while in Cairo, decided to cut short his trip. This surprised his friends for he had earlier intended to return to America after the visit to Egypt. Emma Calve offered to pay his passage back to India and, moved by her generosity, he told her, 'I want to go back to India to die and I want to be with my brothers,' (his brother-monks). When she protested at these words of doom, he told her that he would die on 4th July. Emma bought him a first-class ticket for his voyage back and bid farewell to him with a heavy heart. Thus, Vivekananda set sail for India on 26 November 1900 and reached Mumbai in the first week of December. There were no crowds to greet him on his arrival since he had returned unannounced. Taking a train to Howrah, he arrived at the Belur Math on 9 December to the surprise and delight of the monks.

On his return, Vivekananda received sad news—Captain Sevier had died on 28 October at Almora. Though travel-weary, the monk set out almost immediately for Almora to be with Charlotte Sevier and comfort her on her loss. On his return, he decided to devote some time to his aged mother, Bhubaneswari Devi. The feeling that he had neglected her in pursuing his spiritual mission had troubled him over the years. During his second voyage to the West, he had told Nivedita about the anguish he had caused his mother and his determination to devote the rest of his life to her once he returned. He had earlier remarked to a friend, 'I am no hardhearted brute. If there is any being I love in the whole world, it is my mother.'

While abroad, on 22 November 1898, Vivekananda had written to his dear friend, Raja Ajit Singh of Khetri, asking for financial help for his mother. He said, '. . . to do a service to the world I have sadly neglected my mother.' Then he went on to describe his mother's grief on account of his younger brother, Mahendranath's prolonged absence from home. Travelling all over the world, Mohin had not written to his mother for five years. Knowing that Mohin would probably never be able to earn a living, Vivekananda wanted to make some financial provision for him as well.

Voicing his desire to build a 'little decent home' for his mother, Vivekananda begged his friend for support, saying, 'I am tired, heart-sick and dying—do, I pray, this last great work of kindness to me.' A week later, he wrote to the Raja again requesting him to ensure that the proposed allowance of Rs 100 a month be made permanent so that his mother would continue to get it even after her son's death. Ajit Singh willingly came to his friend's aid and made sure that Bhubaneswari Devi received Rs 100 every month from the Khetri Raj treasury, which she did as long as she lived.

In order to buy his mother a house, Vivekananda borrowed Rs 5,000 from the Math. This was ironic as he was borrowing from that which he had himself earned by driving himself unceasingly without rest or respite. Soon after this, he was involved in a lawsuit for the second time, which an unscrupulous aunt had slapped on him. Presuming that a monk would not pursue a court case, she soon realized that Vivekananda was ready to fight her tooth and nail, and eventually compromised in favour of his family.

Bhubaneswari Devi was now taken on a pilgrimage to some places in Bihar and east Bengal by her eldest son. He also took her to the south, to Rameshwaram. Travelling with her beloved son and visiting these places in his company made her very happy and this gave Vivekananda great satisfaction. Her presence also helped to soothe away his grief over a tragic accident that had befallen his friend, Ajit Singh of Khetri. Apparently the Raja was trying to restore an architectural monument, most probably Akbar's tomb at Sikandra in Agra, at his own expense. He was inspecting a tower when part of it crumbled away and, falling from it, he had died instantly. This was a grievous emotional blow to Vivekananda who spoke of his sorrow in his letters to Sara Bull and Mary

Hale. Now more than ever, he felt that his end was near and said as much to Mary: 'Now I am nearing that *Peace*, the eternal silence.'

Maitreyi, Gargi and tricky questions

Works by ancient Indian grammarians such as Patanjali and Katyayana suggest that women were educated in the early Vedic period. Besides, scriptures such as the Rig Veda and the Upanishads mention several women sages and seers, notably Gargi and Maitreyi.

Of the one thousand hymns of the Rig Veda, about ten are credited to Maitreyi. She is said to have contributed to her husband, Sage Yajnavalkya's knowledge and spiritual growth. The Brihadaranayaka Upanishad relates that when Yajnavalkya wanted to become an ascetic, he decided to divide his possessions between his two wives, Maitreyi and Katyayani. The learned Maitreyi asked whether all the wealth in the world could make her immortal. Yajnavalkya told her that wealth could only make one rich and nothing else. Maitreyi then asked for the wealth of immortality, pleasing Yajnavalkya greatly. He then imparted to her his knowledge of the soul and of attaining immortality.

Gargi was the daughter of Sage Vachaknu and composed several hymns that questioned the origin of all existence. When King Janaka of Videha organized a philosophical debate, she was one of the participants. Sage Yajnavalkya, who had silenced many an eminent scholar and was confident of winning the debate, was astounded

when she fired a stream of questions at him on the immortality of the soul, the arrangement of the universe and many other topics which he did not know the answers to. Shocked and furious, he shouted at her to stop or else her head would fall off! So Yajnavalkya managed to win the debate but Gargi's superior intelligence must have made him feel horribly queasy! Hence, women could clearly become very learned in the Vedic sciences but whether the men wanted to acknowledge this was another matter altogether.

Incidentally, one of Gargi's questions to Yajnavalkya was, 'The layer that is above the sky and below the earth, which is described as being situated between the earth and the sky and which is indicated as the symbol of the past, present and future, where is that situated?' He didn't know the answer to this one. Do you?

11 🜂 The Death of a Giant

In January 1902, Josephine MacLeod came to Kolkata from Japan bringing with her the renowned Japanese artist, Kakuzo Okakura, whom she greatly admired. She took him to the Belur Math to meet Vivekananda and, though his health was still fragile, the latter agreed to accompany them to the places associated with the Buddha, principally Bodh Gaya and Varanasi. To the monk, this was not just to fulfill Okakura's desire but also a way to pay his last homage to the Buddha and to the city that had played such an important role in his earlier travels.

In April 1902, Josephine left for London to attend the coronation of King Edward VII, the son of Queen Victoria. Before she left, she had a very significant conversation with her friend that was to haunt her in later days. They were at the Belur Math watching Sister Nivedita distribute prizes for an athletics event when Vivekananda suddenly said, 'I shall never see forty.' Josephine, knowing him to be just thirty-nine, protested, 'But, Swami, Buddha did not do his great work until between forty and eighty.' Vivekananda merely replied, 'I have delivered my message and I must go.' When Josephine asked why, he remarked, 'The shadow of a big tree will not let the smaller trees grow up. I must go to make room.'

On 2nd July, Vivekananda spent a considerable amount of time with Nivedita even insisting on serving her lunch although he was fasting on that day. When she protested, he laughed and said, 'But Jesus washed the feet of His disciples.' Thereafter, Nivedita submitted, reflecting on how he seemed to be much better. In fact, it was quite probable that he would recover sufficiently to be able to travel to Japan in the autumn and work there.

On 4th July, Vivekananda worked very hard, spending over three hours in meditation, and teaching and conversing with the others all day. In the evening, he went for a walk and covered two miles before returning to his room at the Math. Dismissing everyone on the plea that he wanted to meditate, he sat there awhile before lying down and calling to a boy to fan him because he was tired. Half an hour later, the boy noticed that Vivekananda's hand was trembling and his breathing seemed irregular. The boy immediately shouted for help but when the other monks reached they saw that their master had stopped breathing and was no more. Later, in a letter to Mary Hale, Nivedita noted, 'He left everything in order. Everything at peace and in the moment of his greatest strength, quietly, of his own will, he left us.' He had embraced death that night and just as he had predicted—before the age of forty.

On 5th July, an anguished Nivedita spotted a garment on Vivekananda's bed and asked Swami Saradananda,

'Is *this* going to be burnt? It is the last thing I ever saw him wear!' Saradananda offered her the entire cloth but she only wanted a corner of the border to send Josephine as a keepsake. However, she neither had a knife nor a pair of scissors with her at that point. Moreover, she was not sure whether cutting the garment was an appropriate thing to do under the circumstances. Hence, Nivedita remained still, mourning the tremendous loss of a father figure and watching the unending streams of desolate people who had come to pay their respects to Vivekananda. Meanwhile, the garment was sent away to be burnt. Sometime later, Nivedita felt as if her sleeve had been twitched and, all of a sudden, something blew towards her feet. Looking down, she spotted a piece of the garment of the exact dimensions of two to three inches that she had wanted to cut. It was intact—neither burnt by fire nor blackened by ash. Nivedita was transfixed by this miracle and later told Josephine in a letter, 'I took it as a letter from him to you, from beyond the grave.'

So ended the life of one of the greatest persons of India; one who had once declared, '. . . may I be born again and again, and suffer thousands of miseries so that I may worship the only God that exists, the only God I believe in, the sum total of all souls . . .'

Sister Nivedita and her work

The school for girls that Sister Nivedita started in November 1898, which marked the beginning of her work in India, was in the Bagbazar area of Kolkata. At the time, girls were deprived of even basic education and she would often go from home to home in order to educate them, braving the hostility of some of their male family members. In fact, widows and adult women were also among her students. In her school, she taught sewing, basic hygiene, nursing and so on, apart from holding varied discourses.

Besides this, Sister Nivedita was involved in other social welfare activities. For instance, during the outbreak of a plague epidemic in Kolkata in 1899, she took care of afflicted patients, personally cleaned rubbish from localities and inspired many youths to render voluntary service in this regard. She inserted appeals for help in English newspapers and handed out written instructions for disease-prevention measures in different areas.

Sister Nivedita was a skilled orator and writer, and extensively toured India to deliver lectures on culture and religion. She appealed to the Indian youth to work selflessly for the cause of their motherland along the lines of Swami Vivekananda's ideals. In later years, she took up the cause of India's freedom from the British, motivating people through her lectures. In fact, she had a direct relationship with many of the young revolutionaries of Bengal, including those of Anushilan Samiti, a secret organization.

Among Sister Nivedita's numerous publications, *The Web of Indian Life* is a notable work that sought to rectify many myths regarding Indian culture and customs that were rampant in the West. She also recorded some of her experiences with Swami Vivekananda in *The Master As I Saw Him*.

Sister Nivedita's close friendship with Sarada Devi was one of the abiding aspects of her life in India. In fact, the first-ever photograph of Sarada Devi was apparently taken at her place. The brother-disciples of Swami Vivekananda, too, admired and respected her for her remarkably selfless contribution to the welfare of Indian women and people in general. Accordingly, her epitaph aptly reads: 'Here reposes Sister Nivedita who gave her all to India.'

TRIVIA
TREASURY

Turn the pages to discover more fascinating facts and tantalizing tidbits of history about this legendary life and his world.

WHAT HAPPENED AND WHEN

- **1858**: India is formally taken over by the British Crown.
- **1863**: Vivekananda (Naren) is born in Kolkata in January.
- **1870**: Vivekananda starts his formal schooling at the Metropolitan Institution, Kolkata.
- **1879**: Vivekananda leaves the Presidency College, Kolkata, and joins the General Assembly's Institution (later known as the Scottish Church College). He impresses his professors, particularly his principal, Professor William Hastie.
- **1881**: Vivekananda meets Sri Ramakrishna at the house of Surendranath Mitra and begins his visits to Dakshineswar.
- **1884**: Vivekananda's father, Bisvanath Dutta, dies of a massive heart failure in February.
- **1885**: Sri Ramakrishna moves to a garden-house at Cossipore in December where his young disciples, headed by Naren, nurse him.
- **1886**: Sri Ramakrishna succumbs to cancer and passes away in August. His disciples conduct a ceremony

called *viraja* at Baranagore around the end of the year, take vows of chastity and poverty, and adopt the ochre robe.

- **1888**: Vivekananda leaves Baranagore for Varanasi. Later, at Hathras, he makes Sharat Chandra Gupta his first monastic disciple. He travels around the country calling himself Swami Vividishananda or Swami Satchidananda.
- **1891**: Vivekananda meets Ajit Singh, the Raja of Khetri, in June with whom he forms a bond of friendship and mutual respect.
- **1892**: Vivekananda has a powerful spiritual experience at Kanyakumari at the end of the year and formulates his plan for the future.
- **1893**: Vivekananda is given his title by Ajit Singh in May. He boards the ship on 31 May and reaches Chicago on 30 July. He participates in the Parliament of Religions from 11 September to 27 September and his speeches take the world by storm.
- **1895**: Vivekananda arrives in London from America in September and stays till November.
- **1896**: Vivekananda makes his second visit to London in April and stays there till December. He sets sail for India on the Prinz Regent Luitpold on 16 December.
- **1897**: Vivekananda reaches Colombo in January. He later crosses over to India and finally arrives in Kolkata on 19 February to a tumultous welcome.

On 1 May, Vivekananda establishes the Ramakrishna Mission Association. He later travels and lectures extensively in the cities of north India.

- **1898**: Margaret Noble arrives in Kolkata in January and Vivekananda initiates her into the Ramakrishna Order on 25 March, giving her the name 'Nivedita'. The Belur Math is consecrated on 9 December and becomes the permanent headquarters of the Ramakrishna Order.
- **1899**: Vivekananda sets sail from Kolkata on 20 June on his second visit to the West. He arrives in London on 30 July and leaves for New York on 17 August.
- **1900**: Vivekananda transfers his power over the property and organization of the Ramakrishna Math and Mission to Rakhal and others in succession in August. The trust deeds are executed at the British Consulate in Paris and sent to Kolkata. He gives a speech at the Congress of the History of Religions in Paris in September. Vivekananda later sets sail for India from Egypt on 26 November by an Italian ship, Rubattino, which reaches Mumbai in December. He arrives at the Belur Math on 9 December.
- **1902**: Vivekananda accompanies Josephine MacLeod and a Japanese artist, Kakuzo Okakura, to the places associated with the Buddha, principally Bodh Gaya and Varanasi. He passes away on 4 July.

- **1858**: Minnesota admitted as the thirty-second US state (May), Baron Lionel de is the Rothschild first Jew to be elected to the British Parliament (July).
- **1863**: Emancipation Proclamation ending slavery issued by Abraham Lincoln, the American President (January), Worldwide Red Cross organized in Geneva (October).
- **1870**: Franco-Prussian war begins (July), Italy annexes Rome and Papal States (October).
- **1879**: Zulu war against British colonial rule in South Africa begins (January); Chile declares war on Bolivia and Peru, starting the War of the Pacific (April).
- **1881**: End of First Boer War (March), French troops occupy Algeria and Tunisia (April).
- **1884**: Greenwich established as universal time meridian of longitude (October), British protectorate proclaimed over southeast New Guinea (November).
- **1885**: Louis Pasteur successfully tests an anti-rabies vaccine (July); Ito Hirobumi, a samurai, becomes the first Prime Minister of Japan (December).
- **1886**: Spain abolishes slavery in Cuba (October), Great Britain/Germany divide boundaries in East Africa (October).
- **1888**: National Geographic Society founded in Washington DC (January) the Convention of

Constantinople is signed, guaranteeing free maritime passage through the Suez Canal during war and peace (March/October).

- **1891**: Jews are expelled from Moscow, Russia (April), British Central African Protectorate (now Malawi) forms (May).
- **1892**: Battle at Mengo, Uganda, when French missionaries attack British missionaries (January); First escalator patented by inventor, Jesse W. Reno, in New York (March).
- **1893**: Ivory Coast becomes a French colony (March); the treaty of the Durand Line, which has gained recognition as an international border between present-day Pakistan and Afghanistan, is signed (November).
- **1895**: Cuban war for independence from Spain begins (February), China cedes Taiwan to Japan under Treaty of Shimonoseki (April/May).
- **1896**: First modern Olympic Games officially opens in Athens (April); the last Tsar of Russia, Nicholas II, is crowned (May).
- **1897**: British troops occupy Bida Gold Coast, Ghana (January); the Graeco-Turkish War, also called 'Thirty Days War', is declared between Greece and the Ottoman Empire (April).
- **1898**: Spanish-American War begins (April), China leases Hong Kong's new territories to Britain for ninety-nine years (June).
- **1899**: The Philippine-American War begins

(February), South African Boer Republic declares war on England (October).

- **1900**: Anti-foreigner and anti-West Boxer rebellion begins in China (May/June), British protectorates of Northern and Southern Nigeria established (January).
- **1902**: Cuba gains independence from Spain (May), the Boers and the British army sign peace treaty (December).

VIVEKANANDA LIVES ON . . .

Vivekananda's writings inspired several freedom fighters like Subhash Chandra Bose and Aurobindo Ghose, the former labelling him 'the maker of modern India'. Several Indian leaders and philosophers have also acknowledged his influence. Mahatma Gandhi once noted that Vivekananda's influence increased his 'love for his country a thousandfold'. Vivekananda also inspired Jamsetji Tata, the pioneering Indian entrepreneur and industrialist whom he met on his voyage from Japan to Chicago, to set up the Indian Institute of Science, one of India's finest research institutions today.

Vivekananda's ideas live on in his books *Raja Yoga*, *Karma Yoga*, *Bhakti Yoga* and *Jnana Yoga* that are a compilation of his lectures and are inspirational reading material. A film on his life was also made in 1995 (released in 1998), starring the popular actor, Mithun Chakraborty, as Ramakrishna Paramahamsa and Sarvadaman D. Banerjee as Vivekananda.

As most of Vivekananda's writings concerned the Indian youth, the National Youth Day is celebrated in India on 12 January ever year to commemorate his birth date. It is observed in schools and colleges all over the country with processions, speeches, recitations, youth conventions, seminars, essay-writing competitions and sports events.

Apart from this, many organizations have derived their inspiration from him such as the Vivekananda Youth Forum (VYF) that was formed in 1987 by a group of young individuals who desired to make a difference in society based on his ideas. The VYF imparts formal and non-formal education to the children in slums of Juhu in Mumbai, interacts with street children and identifies children with special needs among other things. Others have adopted his name such as the Vivekananda Study Circle at the Indian Institute of Technology (IIT) at Chennai and the Vivekananda Samiti at IIT Kanpur. There is also the Vivekananda Kendra at Kanyakumari, a thriving Hindu spiritual organization based on the principles he preached.

There are several structures that memorialize Vivekananda's presence. For instance, the Swami Vivekananda Temple in Belur that was built in 1924 marks the spot of his cremation. His room containing articles used by him at different times and places is preserved. Beside the temple stands a *bel* tree in the place of the original one under which he used to sit and near which, according to his wish, his body was cremated. Another structure is the Vivekananda Rock Memorial in Kanyakumari, built in 1970 to commemorate Vivekananda's visit in 1892. It stands on one of two rocks located off the mainland of Vavathurai, India's southernmost tip. On 26 December 2004, when the Tsunami hit India's coast, more than 500 tourists were stranded on this memorial as there were no boats available to bring them back to the mainland.

Another structure that pays tribute to his memory is the Vivekanandar Illam or Vivekananda House in Chennai that marks the place where he stayed for nine days when he visited the city in 1897. It now houses a permanent exhibition on him set up by the Chennai branch of the Ramakrishna Math. Regular youth meetings are conducted here as well. Vivekananda's ancestral house in north Kolkata now functions as an International Research Centre on him. His presence is marked abroad as well. On 11 November 1995, a section of Michigan Avenue, one of the most prominent streets in Chicago, was formally renamed 'Swami Vivekananda Way'.

The Ramakrishna Mission today is a thriving organization with branches all over the country, and with major achievements in the sphere of social work and charity. It has made a mark in the areas of education, healthcare, culture, rural and tribal welfare, and youth movements. The Mission has established many renowned educational institutions in India and has its own colleges, vocational training centres, high schools and primary schools, and teacher training institutes, as well as schools for the visually handicapped. It also involves itself in disaster relief operations during natural and communal disturbances.

Vivekananda's 150th birth anniversary will be celebrated on 12 January 2013. A four-year-long period of celebrations to mark this date was inaugurated in New Delhi on 12 January 2011. The government of India has set up a national committee under the Prime Minister to guide the commemorative events. Apart from approving a film on Vivekananda to be made by the Public Service Broadcasting Trust, the government will also provide a hundred crore rupees to the Ramakrishna Mission to implement various social welfare schemes to celebrate this occasion. A commemorative event will also be held in Chicago.

BOOKS TO READ

Here are some books you can read if you want to find out more about Vivekananda:

1. *Swami Vivekananda—The Living Vedanta* by Chaturvedi Badrinath, by Penguin Books India, 2006.
2. *Vivekananda—A Biography* by Swami Nikhilananda, Advaita Ashrama, Uttarakhand (printed at Kolkata), 1st edition 1964, 24th edition 2010.
3. *Vivekananda—The Man & His Message* by His Eastern and Western Disciples, Advaita Ashrama, Uttarakhand (printed at Kolkata), 8th impression 2010.
4. *A Simple Life of Swami Vivekananda* by Brahmachari Amal, Advaita Ashrama (printed at Kolkata), 4th reprint, October 2007.
5. *The Story of Vivekananda* by Irene Ray and Mallika Clare Gupta, Advaita Ashrama (printed at Kolkata), 16th impression 2010.
6. The Amar Chitra Katha title *Vivekananda* (vol.517)
7. *The Prophet of Modern India: A Biography of Swami Vivekananda* by Gautam Ghosh, Rupa & Co., 2003.

There are many other books on Vivekananda published by the Advaita Ashrama. Information on him is also available on several websites.